The Learning Experiences of Overseas Students

The Learning Experiences of Overseas Students

Edited by Margaret Kinnell

The Society for Research into Higher Education
& Open University Press

Published by SRHE and
Open University Press
Celtic Court
22 Ballmoor
Buckingham MK18 1XW
and
1900 Frost Road, Suite 101
Bristol, PA 19007, USA

First Published 1990

British Library Cataloguing in Publication Data

The learning experiences of overseas students.
  1. Great Britain. Higher education institutions. Foreign
  students
  I. Title   II. Society for the research into higher
  Education
  378'.1982

  ISBN 0-335-09589-5

Library of Congress Cataloging-in-Publication Data

The Learning experience of overseas students/edited by Margaret
  Kinnell.
        p.   cm.
     Includes bibliographical references.
     Contents: The marketing and management of courses/Margaret
  Kinnell—Teaching and learning/Barry Elsey—The student-tutor
  relationship/Joanna Channell—Living needs/Helen Lewins—
  Staff development and training/John Barker.
     ISBN 0-335-09589-5
     1. Students, Foreign—Great Britain.   2. Foreign study.
  I. Kinnell, Margaret.   II. Society for Research into Higher
  Education.   III. Open University Press.
  LB2376.6.G7L43   1990
  370.19'62—dc20   89-39044 CIP

oﬄ 3/93

Typeset by Rowland Phototypesetting Limited
Bury St Edmunds, Suffolk
Printed in Great Britain by St Edmundsbury Press Limited
Bury St Edmunds, Suffolk

Contents

The Contributors and Acknowledgements

John Barker, of the Centre for Extension Studies at Loughborough University, has expert knowledge of post-experience training and staff development in public sector organizations. Also, for several years he has been an overseas students course tutor.

Joanna Channell lectures in the Department of Linguistics at Nottingham University, has been a lecturer in English as a foreign language and has co-authored two textbooks for foreign learners of English.

Barry Elsey is a Senior Lecturer in Adult Education at the Centre for Human Resource Studies, South Australian College of Advanced Education. He taught previously in the Department of Adult Education at the University of Nottingham.

Margaret Kinnell is a Senior Lecturer teaching Management in the Department of Library and Information Studies at Loughborough University.

Helen Lewins is a Lecturer and Course Tutor in the Department of Library and Information Studies at Loughborough University. She has extensive experience of course design and research supervision for overseas students.

We have many organizations and individuals to thank for their help, guidance and co-operation during the research which gave rise to this book. First, we are grateful to the Leverhulme Trust which funded the project – and without the immense co-operation of colleagues too numerous to mention by name, the students and staff of Loughborough and Nottingham Universities, this study would not have been possible. In particular, senior colleagues in our institutions were supportive throughout the period of the research: their active interest in the findings as they emerged was extremely helpful. Similarly, we owe many of the insights into overseas students' needs to the patience and perseverance of our research workers, Julie O'Neill and Pat West. To them we also owe the meticulous collation of a mass of complex and fascinating data. The United Kingdom Council for Overseas Student Affairs, the Nottingham Area Council for Overseas Student Affairs, the Overseas Students Trust and the British Council offered valued information and advice as the study proceeded. Needless to say, any errors in this study are of our making alone.

Not least, families and friends have supported us throughout the lengthy period of the research and writing for this book – to them too, thank you.

Introduction

Barry Elsey and Margaret Kinnell

Background

> Unless you conduct yourselves with more restraint and moderation to-
> wards them [overseas students], they will be driven into abandoning their
> studies and leaving the country, which we by no means desire.

This statement, attributed to Henry III in 1231 and addressed to the inhabi-
tants of Cambridge, demonstrates that seeing overseas students as desirable in
principle but generating problems in practice is by no means a new issue. While
the tradition of students travelling abroad for some part of their education has
been an important continuity in the history of higher education,[1] so too has been
this perception that problems are likely to arise for both the students and the
host country.

Studies of overseas students in Britain, which date from the Lee-Warner
Committee Report of 1907, have largely followed this line of reasoning. Early
welfare organizations had been set up in the late nineteenth century to assist
well-to-do Indian students arriving in the UK.[2] But by 1922 the Lee-Warner
Committee was already looking to a wider brief, namely the need to provide
information on educational matters in the home country and to advise on
educational and financial, as well as welfare matters once in the host country.[3]
While the welfare support offered by voluntary organizations steadily developed in the 1920s and 1930s it was only after the Second World War that
greater concern began to be shown for the 'problems' caused by the influx of
large numbers of overseas students.

Students from developing countries, where comparable higher education was
unavailable, arrived with high expectations of British education and the British
way of life.[4] The social reality they faced, namely prejudice of one kind or
another, was a problem highlighted in several studies undertaken in the 1960s.[5]

To the issues of welfare needs, culture shock and prejudice, had to be added a
further 'problem' – that of language mastery.[6] Several studies during this period
considered overseas students' difficulties with English. For example, when
mainly Commonwealth students were interviewed, it was found that while

language proficiency in itself was not an effective predictor of academic success students did tend to overestimate their ability on arrival and would not admit to difficulties.[7] Specific linguistic problems were also looked at[8] and overseas students were seen to cling to textbooks because in them they found none of the colloquialisms that caused difficulties when listening to lecturers and engaging in discussion.[9] More broadly, the communication problems of overseas students at the North East London Polytechnic as well as technology students at Birmingham and Loughborough universities were considered. While writing essays, speaking, and understanding lectures and tutorials were areas of particular difficulty, language inadequacies in the social context were also important. Even though language courses were set up, the language competencies of overseas students tended to be seen as the problem of students, not their teachers.[10]

A further 'problem' for overseas students, identified in the 1960s, was their approach to learning and teaching. Students perceived a lack of direction from their tutors and did not welcome having scope for planning self-study programmes.[11] They needed more time for reading, listening and writing, preferring to learn from texts and to seek help from friends when necessary; additionally, they did not respond easily to discussion methods when being taught. There was a reliance on rote learning, together with excessive deference to teachers and competitive attitudes to other students when faced with the independent study methods of British higher education.

One response was to offer prescriptive advice for students on adapting to British methods of study, including preliminary instructions on these methods, on study skills, the provision of orientation and supplementary courses and effective supervision.[12] The viewpoint in this and much of the other literature on the problems faced by overseas students was that students were in need of and dependent on the knowledge and education which we in Britain could provide: 'they' had problems with 'our' system (of a socio-cultural, linguistic, academic, or practical nature) which 'we' could help them to overcome. Ownership of the system was largely assumed to rest with the host country.[13]

Consideration was meanwhile being given to the financing of overseas students. Differential fee levels had been introduced in 1967, although in the early 1970s the real cost of fees fell when inflation and a weak pound were taken into account. However, with economic problems, the rise in unemployment, the virtual demise of the Commonwealth and new immigration legislation, the context in which overseas students came to study in Britain altered and questions arose about the purpose of providing this education. Quotas were introduced in 1976, but still numbers continued to rise to an all-time high in 1979, when the very steep rise in fees followed by the sudden introduction of full-cost fees in 1980 caused the numbers to fall away dramatically.[14]

One effect of the far-reaching events of the 1970s was to bring into prominence organizations which had been set up to monitor and further the interests of overseas students. Students' problems had suddenly become an issue for the institutions seeking to recruit them. To the voice of the British Council were added, amongst others, those of the Overseas Students Trust (OST), the

United Kingdom Council for Overseas Student Affairs (UKCOSA), the National Union of Students (NUS) and the World University Service (WUS). All of these commissioned or published material on overseas students. With the publication of the study commissioned by the Overseas Students Trust from the Grubb Institute[15] new light was thrown on the subject of overseas students. Students were found to have expectations of universities as institutions that would cater for all their socio-cultural and practical needs, to the extent that they did not take seriously those comments in publicity material that detailed a reality to the contrary.

Emphasis on the absence of academic guidelines, the overwhelmingly British context of teaching material, a lack of rapport with host students, unsuitable accommodation and a failure to be related to as individuals, were all noted yet again as issues, because the focus of institutions had remained unchanged since the early 1960s – even though commentators from the relevant welfare organizations had sought to shift the emphasis of the debate from student to institutional problems. There was a need to look for root, institutionally based, causes for student 'problems' and then to alter the structure and organization of the services offered.

A further investigation of the learning problems of overseas students[16] then followed, with a close examination of how students' modes of study affected their academic development. The actual organization of written discourse and the patterns of spoken interaction were found to differ. Also, passive understanding of learned problem solutions, using questions for clarification rather than for probing, and an absence of lateral thinking were found to be typical of the learning style of many students. Self-motivation and personal development were being inhibited. Overseas students therefore first had to be helped to discover what they were trying to do when learning in Britain.

Just as the literature began to suggest that a heightened awareness of the issues might produce far-reaching changes which eschewed the 'student problem' approach, an increasing tendency for overseas student decisions to be based on foreign rather than educational policy was noted. Williams[17] instanced the £2300 million spent on overseas services for diplomacy and export promotion in 1981/2; a carefully framed overseas student policy, costing a fraction of this, could have pursued those same objectives and incorporated enhanced educational objectives as well. The fact remained that full-cost fees radically changed the overseas student picture by much more than a drop in numbers.

First, the relationship changed from one of dependency, which evoked paternalistic responses from the host nation, to that of clients paying for services. Financial considerations also led to a change in the pattern of overseas student recruitment, with a steep rise in those from the Middle East and Hong Kong and a decline in those from the Commonwealth, especially its poorer countries. Then, active recruitment by British institutions and heightened publicity, raised the question of overseas numbers on courses, their overall presence in specific institutions, and their preference for certain countries. Meanwhile, the weakening of Commonwealth ties led to reduced comparability of teaching patterns. Some nationalist policies (such as those of Ghana) also tended to create poorer English language competence, which further contributed to the changed nature of the overseas student body. The increasing development of higher education facilities in their own countries also meant that fewer undergraduates and more postgraduates were interested in coming to Britain. Postgraduates were often on contract courses which directed them in nationality groups to specific institutions, or they were on short taught masters' courses often tailored for them alone. This further emphasized the qualification-seeking aspect or 'diploma disease',[18] rather than opportunities for scholarship. Research students, with their particular problems of isolation and the question of the relevance of their research to the home country, together with the increasing presence of the more mature student (often with a family) indicated that the cultural gap between students and their hosts might actually be widening.[19]

The need was now urgent for further reappraisal by receiving institutions. Perhaps it was they rather than the students who had problems? There was still a 'received on sufferance' syndrome in evidence[20] and a comment was made in relation to overseas student recruitment that, 'The British score quite well at the game of international stereotypes. Only personal contact can provide some immunisation against this disease.'[21] Despite this framework of continuing institutional shortcomings universities needed the revenue which overseas students could provide and recruiting was now taking place for financial reasons;[22] revenue generation was an urgent priority.

Given the criticisms levelled at institutional practices, could universities provide education for their customers in ways that met their needs? It was still necessary to itemize the English language needs of overseas students in Cambridge;[23] and in a series of studies at York University[24] it was found that language problems affected not only linguistic competence, there were additional social and cultural implications for students. The lack of understanding by admissions tutors of English language qualifications, or a possible tendency to interpret these in a variety of ways in their desire to recruit, led to some students having little hope of closing the language gap – especially on one-year courses. Despite several initiatives, for example, that of the National Union of Students which produced a pack for Student Union executive members to help them in their dealings with overseas students, a Coombe Lodge Report in 1985 pinpointed a lack of liaison between welfare officers, overseas student advisers, academic staff and those who managed the institutions, which still led to the view that students' problems were related to the individual's failure to cope for a variety of reasons, rather than as a result of institutional practices.[25] A failure to come to grips with institutional responses to overseas students' needs was the crux of the matter, yet this was still not being adequately addressed.

The recent literature shows that UKCOSA in particular has tried to influence change both at government and institutional level, based on first-hand assessment of the situation. It was considered that a structured system of teaching involving pre-term and pre-course orientation and specific course design, offered scope for students to take greater responsibility for their studies in a sequential way.[26] Staff development programmes for experienced as well as new staff which facilitated coping strategies, assisted by outside bodies such as UKCOSA, were recommended.

The question of differences in approaches to concepts of learning, teaching and assessment of overseas students and the importance of cultural bias, had also not been fully considered. It has been argued that there is a causal link between students' perceptions of their learning environment and their attitudes to learning; the student problem-oriented approach of institutions is seen as unhelpful in developing a positive attitude in students.[27] A call for 'responsible recruitment' that takes the views of academic, administrative and welfare staff into account when developing recruitment policies and practices would shift the emphasis much more to the institution's responsibility to pre-empt problems.[28]

The most recent broad investigation of both overseas students and their institutions, for the Overseas Students Trust, drew further attention to the financial context of recruitment, a context which has inescapably played an important part in universities' responses to the question of overseas student recruitment.[29]

Despite the continuing debate on the need for greater awareness of students' needs and a commitment to providing for them, recovery in overseas student numbers particularly at the postgraduate level had certainly occurred, undoubtedly due partly to the intervention of the 1983 'Pym Package' of selective subsidies. Although finance motivated recruitment, the 'hard sell' appeared to be moderating. At least some universities were found to have established a rationale for recruitment based on student experience of academic and social pressures. Student responses in the Overseas Students Trust survey suggested that their needs were beginning to be addressed.

The Next Steps, a follow-up study by the Overseas Students Trust, recommended modest extra funding involving the Department of Trade and Industry and the Department of Employment as well as an extension of support from the Department of Education and Science.[30] Both this report and that by Shotnes emphasized that the funding of essential areas such as induction, orientation and language and proper codes of practice on academic and pastoral care must be addressed. *Consistent* institutional and national policies were called for.

It was in the light of these issues that the research which underlies this book was started. As teachers closely involved with overseas students in our institutions we recognized that the 'problems' posed by recruiting overseas students needed to be addressed in fundamental and positive ways. The negative focus on problems which had dominated the previous literature, rather than the positive aspects of recruitment from the student viewpoint, helped in defining our approach. We wanted to see the needs and expectations of students related to those of institutions in order to move forward the debate on providing for overseas students within UK higher education. Both of the universities in which we worked had a commitment to overseas students based on long experience of teaching and supervising the research programmes of overseas students. It was from this positive platform therefore that we approached the investigation.

Research methods

The thinking behind the research design and methodology used in the study had its origins in the first meeting of what was to become the project team. The common concern of that first meeting was the need to better understand how to teach overseas students effectively. This easily led into complementary concerns with facilitating learning and helping overseas students adapt to a different culture, and from thereon into thinking about the implications of the recruitment policies of our two universities. We could not avoid a problem-centred focus, but, unlike conventional ways of thinking about overseas students, our concerns were about meeting their needs through problem solving approaches to teaching, learning, inter-cultural communication, and effective policies of infrastructure support. Implicit in this thinking was a need to understand the issues from the standpoints of overseas students and university staff: in the former group from students engaged in different kinds of study, and in the latter from senior administrators, academics and a variety of support staff. Although we clearly had sympathetic concerns for the needs of overseas students we deliberately adopted an even-handed approach to the proposed enquiry.

With the full complement of five as the project team the emergent research proposal was accepted by the Leverhulme Trust in 1986. The research project team employed two very able part-time research assistants until near the end of 1987. While based in each university they were in regular communication and personal teamworking throughout the entire project.

The research has some special features which deserve to be highlighted. The first is that it was located in two neighbouring universities of comparable size, both with large science and technology departments, although with a different mix of specialisms in the arts, humanities and social studies. Nottingham University also has a very large Medical School. What they did have in common was an equally energetic commitment to the necessities of income generation, in part through overseas student recruitment. Moreover both universities had from less pressing times a long record of provision for overseas students.

The search for inside knowledge, through the experiences and perceptions of overseas students and university staff, fostered an action research orientation, in so far as it was considered important to issue regular interim reports of research in progress to promote discussion. The onus on action research meant that knowledge outcomes were ideally to be linked to policy circle discussion and, ultimately, translated into staff development programmes, as well as the usual forms of dissemination through academic papers.

Above all, the research was set against regarding overseas students as problem cases, in need of some kind of Band Aid remedy, but rather as integral parts of a changing policy context made up of central government policies for higher education; university policy and especially income generation; teaching and learning approaches employed by academics; staff morale and the nature of the academic role; the quality of infrastructure support services; and, more elusively, attitudes towards overseas students. Such a complex pattern of interaction could not be reduced to a single problem focus, worse still, 'blaming the victim', but necessarily dynamic and changing, conducive to an interpretive, policy-focused approach.

This thinking determined our choice of research methods. The project started officially after the academic year had well and truly begun so that we had to rule out a developmental study. This decision was compounded by the time constraints of the project, which was funded for only two years. Moreover, since some retrospection would be required a fully participative design would also be inappropriate. The survey method was therefore chosen as one means of data gathering on the strength of two key features:

(i) that self-report questionnaires would provide insights into the expectations and experiences of overseas students at the two universities, and

(ii) that the main thrust would be of a phenomenological nature, allowing for individual comment on their expectations and experiences and honouring students' insights as valid.

Practically, self-report questionnaires are quickly and uniformly administered and from the returns by respondents subsamples for interview can be organized. We had to accept the voluntary nature of the survey approach, of course, and that subsampling would be self-selective to all intents and purposes. This caused some problem in that there was a disparity between the response rates at the two universities for one of the surveys. Supporting data from interviews were therefore of considerable importance.

For the other principal means of data gathering, interviews with various categories of university staff (no surveys were attempted), we adopted a different approach, by identifying those in the best position to respond on the basis of role responsibilities and experience. With both staff and students much reliance was placed on personal interviews, mostly of a semi-structured kind, to illuminate thoughts and feelings behind, as in the case of student surveys, matter-of-fact statements and responses to multiple-choice questions.

It was decided not to attempt any control group surveys or interviews with home students. The temptation to do so was understandably strong as our evidence might have appeared firmer. We were also aware that the review of the literature had suggested that some of the experiences of home and overseas students were alike. Pragmatically, we chose not to because control groups would pose difficulties of direct comparability and add little to the setting up of staff development and training. Furthermore, the spirit, if not the letter, of the funding conditions precluded the extra cost of time and money required for control groups. However, a future project might well consider comparing home and overseas students' needs, expectations and learning experiences.

The research project therefore comprised the following stages:

1. Literature review and analysis of the key issues related to overseas students' learning and socio-cultural experiences, as well as policies concerning overseas student recruitment.
2. Pilot survey of overseas students at both universities.

3. Self-report questionnaire survey of overseas students completing their studies in 1986 at both universities.
4. Follow-up interviews of volunteer respondents.
5. Interviews with postgraduate research students.
6. Self-report and semi-structured or 'open-ended' questionnaire survey of new students on their expectations prior to beginning studies at university.
7. Interviews with university staff, at all levels, to elicit their perceptions and experiences of overseas students, covering many aspects of the relationship as well as focused on specific role responsibilities.
8. Collation of results and report writing to final draft.
9. Dissemination (which was also carried out at different interim points of the research).

The particular methodology for each university had to vary slightly according to different circumstances governing accessibility and other practical considerations. These did not affect the overall design of the research.

Throughout the entire project the research team held regular formal planning meetings and maintained a good deal of informal exchange of views and experiences about work in progress. In every respect the project teamwork was a model of co-operation.

Summary of the research findings

As the rest of the book will explore the findings of the research in detail, and their implications for other institutions, only a brief outline is given here of some principal findings. From the data we received from the students we found:

- Pre-arrival communications to students in their home countries were seen as a vital prerequisite to a proper understanding of, first, UK culture and higher education in general, and secondly, the specific institution, its expectations and academic programmes.
- On arrival, suitable permanent accommodation should be available, as soon as students reached the universities. The vacation accommodation needs of students and their special dietary requirements should be more carefully taken into account, as should the needs of mature students with family commitments.
- Appropriate information, advice and help on arrival were important to help create favourable first impressions and to prevent a student's experiences becoming problem-centred. Pre-sessional orientation courses were especially worthwhile.
- Students generally appreciated the good quality of courses and approved the relatively informal lecturing styles; however, the perception that this was an undirected means of teaching created difficulties for some.
- Early contacts with academic tutors seemed to be crucial.
- Many students were concerned with their inadequate English and/or study skills.

- The opportunity to meet and befriend British people, especially other students, was seen as important.

And from the data we gathered from staff we found:

- The institutions saw overseas student recruitment primarily as a way of increasing revenue in the present environment. Financial considerations were uppermost in the minds of decision makers.
- Although 'hard-sell' recruiting was deplored by policy makers, there was some conflict between this and the perceived *need* to recruit.
- The consequences of recruiting overseas students required clearer consideration, in terms of the resources required to provide an adequate support programme.
- The varied educational, cultural, social and personal needs of overseas students were not considered to be sufficiently well met. There was unease that the money from recruiting overseas students was not benefiting them specifically.
- The enormous amount of time required to support overseas students was cited as a key issue, as was recognition for work undertaken by staff in teaching and administering support to students.
- Departmental and individual autonomy could lead to uneven provision. Poor cross-campus communications caused difficulties.
- The lack of a central point of reference for overseas students contributed to problems in co-ordinating support.
- There was felt to be a need for staff training at all levels.

Summary of chapters

In Chapter 1, Margaret Kinnell considers some of the issues raised by overseas student recruitment in relation to managing institutions. She has a particular interest in the marketing of services and has researched and published in this field. Marketing involves much more than 'selling' the institution's services to customers. Analysing how an institution is performing in its marketing strategy is a means to improving its management overall. How institutions should undertake such an analysis, together with the advantages of such an approach, is considered partly by assessing the situations at Nottingham and Loughborough and partly through relating this to the wider picture.

In Chapter 2, Barry Elsey considers the wider context of teaching and learning with overseas students. He has wide experience of adult education, particularly in professional training programmes to Ph.D. level and has broad research interests. In recent years he has travelled extensively in a teaching and consultancy capacity in Australia, China and Europe. It is taken for granted in university adult education that reaching out to the learner, or student-centred learning, is an essential means of enabling adults, who are usually rusty on learning and study skills, to re-engage with intellectual and sustained academic activity in a gentle, relevant and non-threatening manner. The same principles and practices apply in very much the same way to overseas students, many of whom are of mature years. The results of the overseas students' surveys at both universities are examined against this general background of ideas and recent developments.

The focus of Chapter 3 is the one-to-one relationship of overseas students to their individual academic tutors or supervisors. Joanna Channell analyses data obtained from both students and staff to pinpoint the source of some of the dissatisfactions on both sides of that most important relationship. She shows that difficulties follow on logically from mismatches in expectations. Students' expectations of staff are misguided as to the nature of the system of British higher education, whereas staff expectations of students are inappropriate for students who come from a non-British cultural and educational background.

In Chapter 4, Helen Lewins analyses the living needs of overseas students. She describes those concerns identified by the research, including the lack of or inadequacy of pre-arrival information; unfortunate first impressions; problems associated with accommodation, money, food, climate and socialization; and the complexity and lack of co-ordination of the welfare and information agencies which aim to help overseas students.

In concluding, John Barker explores in Chapter 5 how staff development programmes should be implemented. He discusses the context of staff development, and then assesses staff development from the students' and the staff viewpoints. After itemizing the training needs of staff, the organization and implementation of an effective training and development programme is then discussed. The data from the research are used to highlight the training needs of institutions seeking to improve their recruitment practices.

References

1. See, for example, A. Cross, 'Russian students in eighteenth century Oxford', *Journal of European Studies*, 5 (1975), 91–116.
   W. Frijhoff, 'Etudiants étrangers a l'académie d'Angers au 17 siècle', *Lias*, 4 (1977), 13–84.
   W. Frijhoff, 'Etudiants hollandais dans les collèges français aux 17 et 18 siècles', *Lias*, 3 (1976), 301–12.
   G. Stewart, 'British students at the University of Göttingen in the eighteenth century', *German Life and Letters*, 33 (1979), 24–41.
   D. Watt, 'Scottish student life abroad in the fourteenth century', *Scottish Historical Review*, 59 (1980), 3–21.
2. F. Dunlop, *Europe's Guests, Students and Trainees: a Survey on the Welfare of Foreign Students and Trainees in Europe*. Strasbourg, Council for Cultural Co-operation, Council of Europe, 1966.
3. Sir W. Lee-Warner, *Report of the Committee on Indian Students, 1907. Appendix IV of the Lytton Committee Report, Part I*, London, HMSO for the India Office, 1922.
4. Political and Economic Planning, 'Students from the colonies', *Planning*, 20 (1954), 374.
5. Political and Economic Planning, *New Commonwealth Students in Britain*, London, Political and Economic Planning, 1965.

A. Singh, *Indian Students in Britain*, London, Asia Publishing House, 1963.

G. Animashawun, 'African students in Britain', *Race*, 5 (1963), 38–47.

M. Kendall, *Overseas Students and their Families: a Study at a London College*, London, Research Unit for Students' Problems, 1968.

6. A. Livingstone, *The Overseas Student in Britain*, Manchester, Manchester University Press, 1960.
7. A. Sen, *Problems of Overseas Students and Nurses*, Slough, National Foundation for Educational Research, 1970.
8. G. Perren, 'The linguistic problems of overseas students', *ETIC Occasional Paper*, no. 3, London, British Council, 1963.
9. Y. Carlas, 'Some sources of reading problems in foreign language learners', in A. Smith (ed.), *Communication and Culture*, New York, Holt, Rinehart, Winston, 1966.
10. V. Campbell, *Communication Problems of Overseas Students in British Technical Education*, London, N.E. London Polytechnic, 1974.
11. D. Burns (ed.), *Travelling Scholars: an Enquiry into the Adjustment and Attitudes of Overseas Students Holding Commonwealth Bursaries in England and Wales*, Slough, National Foundation for Educational Research, 1965.
12. F. Dunlop, *Europe's Guests, Students and Trainees*.
13. M. Kendall, *Overseas Students in Britain: an Annotated Bibliography*, London, Research Unit for Students' Problems/the United Kingdom Council for Overseas Student Affairs, 1968.
14. P. Williams, *A Policy for Overseas Students*, London, Overseas Students Trust, 1982.
15. B. Reed, J. Hutton and J. Bazalgette, *Freedom to Study: Requirements of Overseas Students in the UK*, London, Overseas Students Trust, 1978.
16. British Council, *Study Modes and Academic Development of Overseas Students*, London, British Council, 1980.
17. P. Williams, *A Policy for Overseas Students*.
18. R. Dore, *The Diploma Disease*, London, Unwin Education Books, 1976.
19. J. Wright, *Learning to Learn in Higher Education*, London, Croom Helm, 1982.
20. Ibid.
21. Sir J. Burgh, *Why Britain Needs Overseas Students*, Speech delivered at Newcastle University, 19 November, 1984.
22. D. Walker, 'Hard-sell recruiting by British universities assailed', *Chronicle of Higher Education*, 30 (1985), 39–40.
23. G. Geoghegan, *Non-native Speakers of English at Cambridge University*, Cambridge, Bell Education Trust, 1983.
24. I. Lewis, *The Student Experience of Higher Education – University of York*, London, Croom Helm, 1984.
25. J. Findlayson (ed.), 'Developing a policy for recruiting overseas students', *Coombe Lodge Report*, 17 (1985).
26. S. Shotnes (ed.), *The Teaching and Tutoring of Overseas Students*, London, United Kingdom Council for Overseas Student Affairs, 1985.
27. J. Wright, 'The acquisition of research skills by postgraduates in UK universities: cognitive development in interactive settings', *Canadian Journal of Counselling*, April 1986.
28. A. Barty, 'Meeting the needs of overseas students', *AUT Bulletin*, May 1985, 18.
29. G. Williams, M. Woodhall and U. O'Brien, *Overseas Students and their Place of Study. Report of a Survey*, London, Overseas Students Trust, 1986.
30. Sir K. Berrill, *The Next Steps. Report of an Advisory Committee of the Overseas Students Trust*, London, Overseas Students Trust, 1987.

1

The Marketing and Management of Courses

Margaret Kinnell

Introduction

In universities which have a long tradition of educating students from abroad, it is only recently that the 'issue' of recruiting overseas students has arisen. Before the introduction of full-cost fees, overseas students were recruited on grounds other than the financial benefit to institutions. In common with most other tertiary institutions, Loughborough and Nottingham universities have been under pressure to recruit increasing numbers of overseas students for financial, as well as the less easily quantifiable educational and cultural reasons that had been a principal motivator in the past. Government is now actively encouraging institutions to recruit students as a means of enhancing their resources and the Jarratt Report specifically pointed to overseas student recruitment as 'a valuable source of income' – immediately prior to warning that universities are 'likely to continue to experience restricted funding for some time'.[1] The message is clear: overseas students are a valuable source of income and should be strenuously cultivated for recruitment. Inevitably, therefore, universities must look to the most effective means of enhancing their recruitment activities, managing the teaching and research programmes of overseas students and organizing those services that support recruitment and teaching.

Despite the significance of the financial rewards, there are, however, important considerations for this overall management of institutions. The Jarratt Committee also sounded a note of caution: 'Universities must, however, ensure that they are not being subsidised from other income.'[2] Their comment that overseas students 'can often be educated at marginal cost to the university' is one that we shall return to, but the implications are clear enough. While enhanced fees provide a powerful incentive to recruiting additional numbers of overseas students, the overall cost structure, as well as the educational and cultural community of the university, must also be considered. The cost of services provided for overseas students should not be allowed to outstrip the financial benefits to institutions.

There is on the other hand a sound commercial argument, as well as important ethical considerations, in ensuring that students receive good value for money. Satisfactory services must be provided to meet students' needs, or they will simply not continue to come to the UK for their higher education. This tension between ensuring that universities enhance both their income and the cultural life of the institution from the recruitment of overseas students, and not wastefully increasing their expenditure on teaching and support services or failing to satisfy students' expectations, lies at the heart of the management function in relation to overseas students in universities. The resolution or at the least the minimizing of this tension, will be the subject of this chapter. The experiences of Loughborough and Nottingham universities will be used to explore the issues and to consider how marketing and management practices might meet the needs of institutions in dealing with them.

The management problem

The management problem facing universities comprises several features. First of all there is a need to consider overseas students as consumers, within an increasingly competitive situation for institutions. There is in addition a range of important environmental influences to be assessed, in order to make sense of the systems that are relevant to overseas student recruitment. The decision to adopt a marketing approach to the management problem largely resulted from this initial exploration of the various factors inherent in the situation. In essence, successfully managing overseas student recruitment was perceived as a marketing problem in writing this chapter. Marketing was not viewed as merely 'promoting' courses to overseas students. On the contrary, it has been seen as axiomatic throughout the analysis that marketing embraces a range of management functions, including:

● assessing the institutions' strengths and weaknesses in relation to provision for overseas students
● analysing environmental influences on overseas student recruitment
● understanding the nature of the relevant markets and publics
● analysing overseas students' needs
● assessing the nature and strength of the competition
● defining organizational objectives in relation to overseas students
● analysing the institutions' services (and products) for overseas students
● designing courses and research programmes to meet the needs of overseas students
● determining fees, costs and the administrative structures to implement financial controls
● deciding on effective support services
● promotion and publicity[3]

This wide-ranging agenda also involved critically evaluating the various systems concerned in the recruitment and management of overseas students. To facilitate such an analysis a Marketing Audit and Marketing Activity Review were undertaken. These marketing models were sufficiently flexible to allow of adaptation to meet the needs of the analysis of practices at Loughborough and Nottingham while at the same time indicating the major issues that needed to be addressed by other university managers.[4,5] Although not an ideal means of considering the problems associated with overseas student recruitment, they served as useful analytical tools in assessing what the institutions were doing and how they could plan for the future.

Marketing audit

Environmental influences on recruitment

The external and internal environments in which universities function are a key factor in the recruitment of overseas students. The policy of assiduously recruiting students, from the late 1970s up to the present, came about as a direct result of environmental pressures, and the management of overseas student recruitment can only be fully understood if seen in relation to these environments. A useful model is given in Figure 1.1 – one which acknowledges the complexity of environmental factors and has the added advantage of providing a means of relating the 'marketing mix' to the environment;[6] from an initial analysis of the environment one can proceed to assess the features of an appropriate marketing mix.[7] (Alternative models of international marketing were considered less helpful as they took insufficient account of the complex nature of the environment surrounding the recruitment process.[8])

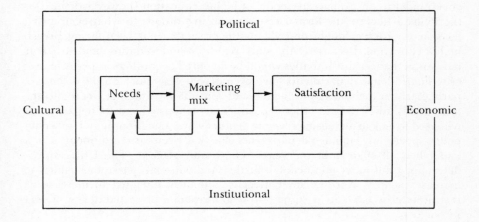

Figure 1.1

The external environment

The external environment in which British universities are operating comprises several complex features that have a direct bearing on the management of overseas student recruitment. First, a demographic trend which is resulting in fewer 18-year-olds forced universities to reconsider their traditional market for undergraduate entry. Secondly, the expansion of higher education, which had seemed so inexorable following the Robbins Report of 1963, has not been sustained: owing not only to the falling birth-rate, but also due to a consistent policy during the last ten years of retrenchment in higher education and financial stringency throughout the public sector.[9] Loughborough and Nottingham universities, like others, have prepared *Academic Plans* in line with the recommendations of the Jarratt Report. These are a means of assessing responses to this challenging (or threatening, depending on one's viewpoint) political and economic environment. In their Plans, the impact of reduced resources is clearly articulated. Academic posts will be lost or frozen; structural changes that include the closing of one department (History at Loughborough) and the merging of others will be required to achieve the rationalization of resources. Some of these structural changes have already been implemented, others – particularly the loss of academic posts – are due to take effect over the next few years as 'natural wastage' occurs.

It is important in understanding how threats from beyond the universities have influenced thinking on student recruitment, to comprehend the impact of the Plans within the institutions. Taken with a range of other pressures – new arrangements for funding through the University Funding Council (UFC); the recent Research Selectivity Exercise; trans-binary studies of some subject areas; disputes between staff and employers on salaries; appraisal schemes and restructuring at the national level; together with the projected move by government to an 'American' model of higher education (however defined) – the Plans articulate the formal responses of institutions to what even a dispassionate observer might describe as the crisis that has been facing British higher education. Because of the stark reality of underfunding, and the clear indication that certain activities would be favoured over others as performance criteria, academic departments have been placed very much on the defensive, particularly in the matter of research and consultancy funding; where income from this is lower than in other departments, obviously heads of departments will need to look to increasing revenue in other ways. Loughborough University policy specifically enjoined departments to look to overseas recruitment, which had fallen off slightly in the years 1985/6 and 1986/7: 'The University is determined not to let numbers fall further and will make strenuous efforts to increase them.'[10] Nottingham University similarly intended to increase its recruitment by 9.9% in 1989/90 – to help forestall a projected deficit of over £1,000,000.

The external pressures which have resulted in these responses are being experienced throughout tertiary education in the United Kingdom; a situation that faced American universities and colleges some ten years ago. They did likewise – in deciding that overseas students should fill places to supplement institutional resources.[11] Australian universities too have encountered problems and have also begun to co-ordinate their policies on recruiting foreign students.[12] The conference on 'International Comparisons in Overseas Student Affairs' highlighted that these same concerns were being experienced by universities in many other countries.[13] In addition to those environmental pressures which are compelling universities in the UK to consider means of generating additional revenue, there should be added the influence of external agencies such as the British Council, the Association of Commonwealth Universities and overseas governments. Their funding gives them considerable weight with universities.

The internal environment

The external environment has then to a considerable extent conditioned the ways in which the internal environment, or 'culture', responds to the question of overseas student recruitment. The formal evidence of Loughborough's and Nottingham's cultures is given in their Plans. Overseas students were clearly linked rather to remedying the financial situation, than being seen as a significant feature of future academic development, with the financial future in both universities a major preoccupation of most members of staff. However, it would be misrepresenting these complex organizations to suggest that their richly varied cultures, made up of diverse and competing interest groups, responded monolithically. While the Plans are its public expression, policy implementation is dependent on how these groups and, most crucially, how individuals perceive the situation. The roles that people see themselves performing, together with very considerable personal and professional commitment, have a significant impact on the ways in which they respond to policy decisions and their performance of duties in relation to overseas students.

Both universities had formal committees to implement policy on overseas student recruitment – Loughborough's Inter-School Working Party on the Recruitment of Overseas Students and the Senate Committee for Overseas Student Recruitment at Nottingham. There were also structures concerned with welfare provision – a subcommittee of the Welfare Committee at Loughborough and the largely student-run Overseas Student Bureau at Nottingham. Both universities operated incentive schemes for departments, to enlist co-operation in recruiting overseas students. Mention should therefore be made of the importance of departmental organizational structures. In both universities the academic departments are largely autonomous units, with heads of department having very real control over the decisions their departments take in relation to student recruitment.

Publics and markets

The main 'client publics' of a university are its prospective students, current students and employers: while 'general publics', including the local community, parents of students, and competitors are also relevant as groups having influence on student recruitment, the client publics are most important for the effective recruitment of students.[14] Prospective students could in theory come from virtually any country: in practice, however, students at both Loughborough and Nottingham came predominantly from Africa, South-East Asia and the Middle and Far East. Agencies having a direct impact on the make-up of the prospective student population included the British Council, the Association of Commonwealth Universities, charitable trusts who sponsored students, and the governments of students' own countries. Employers were also significant, as they frequently sponsored students; sometimes the foreign government was also the employer. Current and past students were similarly of tremendous importance: their view of the university, transmitted home, created lasting impressions.

A further dimension to these publics is the network of interactions taking place between them. The British Council, through its marketing activities, plays an important role in influencing foreign governments' decisions on sending students to the UK. Central government is also one of the most significant of these influences, by its policy on fees as well as by the impact of wider economic and political decision-making on relations with sponsoring governments.

Local communities also play their part in forming the perceptions of prospective students and their sponsors as to living and studying in Britain. One of the more disturbing findings of the Overseas Students Trust survey of *Overseas Students and their Place of Study*, was that a quarter of all overseas students felt they had been badly treated during their time in Britain.[15]

Both Loughborough and Nottingham had strong links with certain countries – targeting of specific areas appeared to be well-developed – for example, Nottingham's links with Hong Kong in providing a tailor-made bridging course for education students and Loughborough's water engineering course for developing countries. In addition the universities also pursued markets that have been identified by the British Council as particularly reliable providers of students – a further indication of the Council's importance in the development of a marketing strategy. It should be noted that the British Council's prime aim in its marketing activities is 'the winning of friends for Britain: trade, aid and influence in the broadest sense'.[16] Their valuable series of market surveys was intended to bolster the government's full-cost fees policy, rather than assisting any one sector or institution within higher education. Quite specifically, they were given £100,000 in 1983 to fund a marketing adviser's post and to develop a marketing strategy. Market surveys were therefore conducted in those countries considered most likely to be of importance for wide-ranging purposes, political as well as economic: Singapore, Indonesia, Brunei, South Korea, Thailand, Jordan, Algeria, Japan, China. General recruitment and promotional visits were then made by British academics to the follow-up educational 'fairs' based on local Council offices – at which both Loughborough and Nottingham were represented.

Local collaboration had also begun – Nottingham University and Trent Polytechnic had already joined forces to promote Nottingham as a place to study, and further joint promotion ventures were planned. It was notable, however, that in both Nottingham and Loughborough Universities much of the recruiting was achieved by the initiatives of individual departments; admissions tutors were targeting additional markets as a result of professional contacts of one kind or another. Paradoxically, such a broad approach which has evolved over the years and is based not only on 'pure' marketing principles but also on sound educational and cultural reasons, might ensure that some of the pitfalls of a marketing drive are avoided. American experience during the late 1970s was of institutions appearing 'subject to the "trading stamp syndrome"–because the competitor down the street is doing it, we probably can't afford not to'.[17] The overseas student markets identified by both Loughborough and Nottingham universities appeared to be diverse enough to counteract this tendency, despite the shift towards a more carefully delineated marketing approach.

Overseas students' needs and perceptions

Having considered the influences of the environment on recruitment, and assessed the nature of the market being targeted by the institution, a marketing audit must turn to an investigation in greater detail of the needs of that market, as identified by the overseas students themselves. Students' perceptions of their experiences were a major part of this research; they were considered to be particularly important, as the literature on overseas student recruitment had largely overlooked the value of clients' perceptions of their learning and living experiences in a British university. The most relevant previous British study, the Overseas Students Trust survey of 1986,[18] had not attempted more than a wide-ranging assessment of student satisfaction or dissatisfaction with their time in UK tertiary education. Broad issues such as racism were touched on, but the very nature of such a survey meant that an in-depth assessment of how students *felt* about a particular university could not be developed.

Overseas students completing their studies

The emphasis in analysing students' needs lay with this component of the data; this first survey (questionnaires and interviews) outlined the major issues, which were later supported by findings from the interviews with research students and the surveys of students' expectations when beginning their studies.

The initial questionnaire was designed to elicit students' feelings about their experiences at Loughborough and Nottingham – including: receipt of prior information; teaching and tutoring approaches; language issues; study methods; sources of academic and personal guidance; accommodation; orientation issues; contacts with British students and level of fees – making up a wide range of concerns involving most of the students' contacts with the institutions. Many of these areas will be dealt with in greater depth in later chapters. However, it is important to outline the major issues at this point, in order to consider their significance for the marketing strategies required of universities.

1 *Receipt of prior information*

At Loughborough it was interesting that the students' responses on 'information received' varied from student to student, largely because the information was not sent as one package, which caused some confusion. The speed with which information was despatched was also seen as important, both in answering initial enquiries and also to provide adequate pre-arrival information. The anxieties produced when facing the totally unknown were thought to be underestimated and there was some general criticism about non-acknowledgement of letters, receipt of money, confirmation of arrangements and so on. Both universities produced information specifically targeted at overseas students; brochures and videos offering information about the campuses had recently been upgraded. Nevertheless, it was stressed that details of British habits, especially eating habits and foods, and of the British system of personal responsibility for learning, together with information on how overseas students might expect to be aided on arrival, would all help to alleviate anxiety. The information sent out by the British Council was consistently praised but was generally available only to the recipients of its sponsorship. Clear, appropriate and timely pre-course communications appeared to be a vital first step in establishing a good relationship with the institution. It should also be stressed that information about the universities came from a wide range of informal communication links as well and that these were highly influential in determining which university was chosen by a student. 'Close friends' studying at a university and the reputation of 'a well-known supervisor' figured in some students' choices, as did the reputation of the university as a whole – image was important. The strong reputation of British higher education was similarly a significant aspect of this image.

2 *Teaching and tutoring approaches*

As the type of course offered by the institution was one of the most important factors for students, inevitably teaching and tutoring approaches were of tremendous importance to them. This was what they had come to experience. Many of the comments on teaching methods, the usefulness of handouts, and so on, could apply equally to home students – it appeared that any problems in teaching quality encountered by British students were more keenly felt by overseas students. This was particularly marked when considering overseas students' perceptions of their study skill needs. The orientation courses offered on both campuses were seen to be particularly valuable in anticipating students' language and study problems and in helping them to settle speedily into the learning environment.

Some interviewees felt with hindsight that the orientation course was so important that it should have been compulsory and free, covering not only language but also practical topics like finding your way about, finance, shopping, the students' union, social customs and use of the library and computer centre. Academic orientation could also properly be arranged departmentally at the start of courses.

Despite general satisfaction with course content (although not always with course *organization*), questionnaire returns concerning academic advice and feedback showed a more varied response.

Constructive feedback was seen to be crucial before students could judge their performance and thus know how to proceed. The actual arrangements for academic tutorial help were also the subject of many comments. The early establishment of a rapport through the tutor first going to the student and expressing genuine interest, involvement and warmth was seen as vital before work could be discussed. Research students particularly commented on the importance of an interactive relationship between the supervisor and the student, which they felt should receive more emphasis.

It was this area of academic help and feedback which appeared to be one of the most important for overseas students, together with effective formal tuition. However satisfactory the content of curricula and the class contact they received these had to be supplemented by sensitive personal support.

Academic support services were similarly seen as vital to a student's success and were also therefore discussed with interviewees; questionnaire respondents also had suggestions.

3 Language issues

Interviewees were asked about their experiences in using English, and several suggestions were also received via the questionnaire returns. For some interviewees language obviously loomed very large. Several non-native speakers were using English as their third language and it was generally agreed that the basic language qualification which students had been obliged to obtain (an ELTS score of around 6.5) was of little value in itself when coping with an academic higher education course. In practice, many students offered an 'O' level English Language pass to fulfil entry requirements. All felt that their English competency had needed to go far beyond this level and they had most often achieved this through daily usage. One criticism of the British Council's orientation/language course was its generalized nature. It was considered that a course more specifically subject-oriented would have been more useful. It was felt that English language provision by departments could be helpful: for example, students who had undergone pre-M.Sc. courses had a compulsory

English module within their course, and programmed texts had formed part of the course for some civil engineering students.

Whereas students would have liked still more tolerance of language problems, they generally found people quite patient with imperfections.

4 *Study methods*

Respondents had, almost without exception, come directly from an environment which had involved either full-time or part-time study, whether from school or from other universities, so they had not experienced difficulty over the actual process of returning to study. Student profiles were different across the campuses – Loughborough had many more one-year postgraduate students than Nottingham.

Many interviewees mentioned the mutual-help method as having been part of their past as well as their present mode of studying and this seemed to take place with whoever was on the same course, regardless of nationality. Informal discussions and exchanges went on all the time amongst the postgraduates.

Time constraints were mentioned many times. Many of the one-year masters' courses were extremely concentrated – although students seemed to prefer the idea of constant study for a shorter time in order to gain the qualifications they were seeking. The study methods undertaken were comparable with those of home students. However, many overseas students were unfamiliar with some types of studying: 15% said that research was new to them, while 10% also noted that writing essays and reports was unfamiliar. About a quarter of respondents agreed that they had difficulty with one or more of these study types. There was a general expectation amongst students that they would need to study constantly in order to succeed and a determination to tackle new study methods positively, including discussion-based learning as well as solitary study techniques.

5 *Sources of academic and personal guidance*

It was clear from the response that in both universities there were neither cross-university policies nor practices regarding personal tutors – although at Nottingham Faculty Advisers for Overseas Students had been appointed to co-ordinate faculty responses to students' problems. Some students had a personal tutor who was also their academic tutor, some had two separate tutors and some had no personal tutor. The need for personal tutors to approach students and establish a sensitive one-to-one relationship in the early days was stressed. This helped to relieve feelings of disorientation. It was considered that once this relationship had been established, needs could be voiced naturally during conversation and students would feel free to seek help. There were pleas for improvements in the handling of personal relationships within the departmental structure.

6 *Accommodation*

Many of the questionnaire suggestions and many of the comments offered by interviewees concerned accommodation. For an overseas student, settling in to appropriate accommodation appeared to be absolutely crucial before they could get down to their work. Many interviewees felt more emphasis should be given to the fact that for most overseas students their university accommodation was their only British base – the requirement that some students move out of their rooms during vacations had taken many by surprise and had proved disconcerting. They had felt transient and disoriented. Accommodation was perceived as a problem by students on both campuses – particularly for postgraduates. There was little specific provision for them and no married quarters available on the campuses. Undergraduates were much better served. There was felt to be a lack of awareness of how short one year is to settle, achieve and reorientate for postgraduate course students. Research students in particular stressed how important it was to them to have a reasonable and quiet place to relax in once they had left their department after long hours of concentrated work. Interviewees generally felt that overseas students were now looking for a 'total package'. Informal information networks quickly passed round news of those institutions which offered good, reasonably priced accommodation, and students expressed the view that they were now in a buyer's market and would see colleagues being selective in future about where they would study.

7 *Orientation issues*

Pre-sessional orientation courses were offered by both universities, although take-up was limited and research students in particular felt the need for more carefully targeted orientation, as they arrived at varying times in the academic year and so missed the early courses.

The Student Counselling Service at Loughborough also organized social events throughout the year, but it was felt this did not meet the need for greater efforts to introduce students to the range of facilities on campus and to life in Britain.

Those students who had attended pre-sessional orientation courses found them extremely helpful and it was felt they should be offered as part of a 'package' for overseas students rather than as an extra.

For postgraduate-course students orientation was also a particular difficulty. Assumptions were made, it was felt, that they should be able to cope because of their mature status, yet they felt as vulnerable as many undergraduate students – especially as many had left families at home to manage without them for a year or more.

8 *Contacts with British students*

The questionnaire returns showed that the majority of the respondents were taught mainly with overseas students and almost half studied outside the classroom also with other overseas students; opportunities for mixing with home students were therefore limited. Breaking down barriers was considered difficult both with British students and indeed the British in general, and this made some students feel very lonely. Hopes that language improvement, cultural understanding and wide-ranging discussion would be set up through friendships with British students were not generally realized. British students tended to socialize in pubs and campus bars. Some overseas students did not drink or were used to a more formal social life which further limited their chances of mixing. There was no doubt that the preponderance of the work ethic for overseas students also limited their social opportunities. Scarcely any of the interviewees had been invited to a British home except possibly that of their tutor, and many not only found this strange but in direct contrast to their prior experiences in such countries as America, the USSR and India where, as foreign students, they had been frequently welcomed to the homes of the indigenous population.

9 *Level of fees*

Throughout, from the surveys of students it was clear that they were conscious of the high fees either they or their sponsors were paying – and most felt strongly about this. There was resentment expressed by some at the attitude that overseas students were welcomed primarily for their fees: 'my Department would take a donkey if it paid overseas students' fees' was the comment of one research student who raised questions about the quality of some of his fellow overseas students.

The cost of fees, together with the high costs of coming to live in Britain served to heighten expectations. As one undergraduate remarked: 'As an overseas student in England I think I have paid tremendously. Therefore in return I am expecting quite a lot.'

Students' needs therefore spanned the whole range of their learning and living experiences as members of the university communities. While they liked the relevance of most courses, the facilities of the campuses (sport at Loughborough and the beauty of Nottingham's campus, in particular) and the quality of course content they disliked the lack of personal attention and feedback from staff, the problems they encountered with language difficulties, the lack of suitable accommodation for postgraduate students and few contacts with home students and the British culture. It was apparent from all the findings that the traditional emphasis on course and research activities, as a means of attracting overseas students to British universities was by no means the only factor that should be considered in developing a marketing strategy. Students were primarily interested in academic attainment, but their broader living needs and their expressed desire to benefit much more widely from their stay in Britain featured prominently in their perception of the institutions.

As Kotler argues, 'the college marketing process starts before the work of the admissions office and continues beyond the work of the admissions office'.[19] 'Taking a position' in the market-place at present requires universities to plan a portfolio that truly meets the needs expressed by students.

Competitors

Until 1979, when the imposition of full-cost fees made UK higher education less financially attractive to overseas students, British universities enjoyed a steady influx of students. Competition was perceived to be much more between British universities, rather than between Britain and other overseas countries. Neither was there the sense of competition from an overwhelming financial incentive for institutions in having large numbers of foreign students. It is only in the 1980s that universities have come to see themselves as operating within an overtly and fiercely competitive situation, a situation to which some institutions have more readily responded than others. With their technological and industrial links, a business-oriented tradition, and reputations for quality in teaching and research, Loughborough and Nottingham might be considered better placed than many universities for the development of a competitive strategy. Nevertheless, their numbers of overseas students had fallen over the last two years because of competition coming first from other countries and secondly from other British institutions.

A major source of competition comes from American colleges and universities. For example, the Jordanian Ministry of Education released figures which showed that the number of Jordanians studying in the United States more than doubled at a time when the British figures were static.[20] An important factor was simply the enormous range of different institutions, giving students and their sponsors a good spread of academic levels, for students of varying abilities. America is also the 'market leader' for Thai students, partly due to a substantial Thai population in the USA.[21] Japan is also entering the market, and offering large amounts of aid, 'in the expectation of long-term gains in terms of influence and future custom'.[22] Australia is another growing competitor; its share of the private undergraduate market is increasing in Singapore.[23] While it is difficult for any one university to adopt marketing and promotional programmes to meet the challenge of such growing competition, taking advantage of the marketing opportunities offered by organizations like the British Council would seem to be essential. Further, a sharper awareness of the strength of the opposition, through exploiting their information sources, will play a part in developing an effective strategy.

The competition from other British institutions is at present largely based on grounds other than fees. However, this is likely to change as universities become increasingly autonomous in their fee-charging policies. For students coming to Britain, overwhelmingly the choice of Loughborough or Nottingham rather than any other UK institution was because of the kind of course offered. The quality of teaching and reputation of departments obviously played a consider-able part in influencing students and their sponsors over their choices. Some students offered the comments that the British Council had recommended them to a department for a particular course. The Department of Library and Information Studies at Loughborough, for example, received many of its overseas students for masters' courses as a result of such recommendations.

Competition is therefore largely on subject lines, with departments having recognized competitors in their own fields. Again, accurate assessment of the competition is likely to become ever more important in developing an effective marketing strategy.

It would seem essential for management at all levels in the universities to take account of the needs expressed by students, as a means of assessing to what extent they compare with these competitive threats from outside. The salient factors noted by students could be seen as adding value to the product offering. Certainly good accommodation, language teaching facilities, well-organized courses, and the whole range of learning and living needs noted as important to students can be compared with what is on offer elsewhere – abroad as well as in Britain.

Organizational objectives

In ascertaining whether an organization is well positioned in the market, the first task must be to clarify the organization's long- and short-term objectives. Because of the difficulty of specifying clear objectives in broad terms, a hierarchy of objectives clarifies the priorities a manager needs to be aware of – no organization can achieve everything at once. An effective marketing audit should therefore raise questions about the appropriateness of the objectives of the organization in relation to the environment in which it operates.[24]

Educational institutions are experiencing especial difficulties at present in framing clear objectives, precisely because the environment is both threatening and turbulent: goals are being set by government which radically affect universities' long- and short-term objectives – goals which may change as the political climate shifts.

Overseas student recruitment has to contribute to the agenda set for universi-ties by political decision-makers – or at any rate this appears to be the way in which policy on overseas student recruitment is largely perceived by university managers, from the evidence of their Plans.

The emphasis on financial constraints in setting objectives for institutions is clearly expressed in the literature. Armenio discussed the problem that American higher education faced of a likely 46% decline in the number of college-age students from 1980 to 1990 and the need for the implementation of 'a full-scale, integrated marketing approach to the admission of international students'. The alternative would be 'continued retrenchment, financial instabil-ity, and possible bankruptcy for many colleges and universities'.[25] Cowell identified a similar concern within the UK public-sector institutions: polytechnics were also concerned that 'time is short and resources limited'.[26] Litten, while realistic in his assertion that 'we have been marketing higher education and its institutions for many years', also acknowledges the new impetus caused by financial constraints – again with reference to American institutions.[27] Mackey is perhaps the most concerned of the commentators on the relationship between financial pressures and marketing 'hype' in her damning indictment of the practices of some impecunious American colleges in the 1970s, 'the decade of dwindling enrollments and budgetary gloom'.[28] Of the eight countries discussed in *International Comparisons in Overseas Student Affairs* it was notable that only West Germany and India had a liberal attitude to fee levels for overseas students; other countries appeared to see such students as a means of higher education earning revenue to subsidize institutions, although there were other considerations as well. The Republic of Ireland and the Netherlands offered help to students from some developing countries as one means of giving overseas aid.[29]

Nevertheless, although a prime objective of universities may be defined in these largely financial terms, other, less overtly stated, objectives also pertain. These are embedded in the ethos of universities: advancing knowledge, wisdom, understanding and professional competence are what most academics see as their professional roles. It is not surprising therefore that in addition to helping universities balance their books, overseas student recruitment is also viewed by the people who implement policy at the departmental level in much more broadly academic terms. Institutional objectives and those of the individuals who must interpret and apply them thus become merged. The perceptions of university staff of their relationships with overseas students largely bore out this view. While financial considerations were an important stated objective, a range of other professional objectives emerged. Staff shared a common belief in the importance of overseas students for the cultural life of their institution. It is important to stress therefore the difficulties in setting out a clear hierarchy of objectives. While universities are obviously concerned with balancing the books, they are also composed of coalitions and individuals whose concern for the academic mission of the institution is an important priority. Reconciling these objectives would appear to be an urgent task.

Marketing System Review

As a means of relating the needs of students to universities' responses, an analysis of the marketing 'systems' forms a further important phase of the marketing audit. The complex systems operating in Loughborough and Nottingham were defined from interviews with those staff identified as having the closest involvement in recruiting and dealing with overseas students. The functions considered included:

Recruitment
Pre-arrival administration

Arrival procedures
Academic provision
Academic support
Language provision
Non-academic and welfare support
Social provision

Their significance for an overall institutional marketing strategy was seen as especially interesting.

1   *Recruitment*

Despite the existence of centralized university committees to look at overseas student recruitment separate departmental initiatives still continued, and there seemed to be some ambivalence between the directive approach already observed in the Academic Plans and the apparent freedom of departments to respond as they wished. A public relations approach had been encouraged and much of the promotional literature had been rewritten. However, evidence that recruitment policies were not being co-ordinated across campus came to light through the interviews and some reservations were also expressed by interviewees about the 'hype' surrounding these approaches, although senior managers insisted that getting the right students was the crux of the campaign.

The question of entry standards was also referred to many times. Policy makers insisted that standards must not be sacrificed in the desire to recruit. However, departmental attitudes were sometimes at variance. Some of the tutors interviewed made pleas for more stringent checks on, for example, language ability.

The view that academic criteria alone were insufficient as a guide to students' likely success was also raised.[30] Staff were also concerned that the services marketed to overseas students and the ability to provide them, did not necessarily equate. Support services should adequately meet students' needs in order to protect future recruitment through providing satisfied customers.

In their task of filling available places with the best applicants admissions tutors worked under a variety of conflicting pressures. They had university standards of entry and English qualifications, plus departmental standards of entry to maintain, and yet at the same time had to balance these demands with the expectation of recruiting as many overseas students as practicable; they had the problem of trying to maintain standards and adhering to their own guidelines while seeing students 'lost' to other universities and polytechnics who might be operating with lower standards of entry and no English language requirements; they had to cope with the unfairness of turning down well-qualified home students who would have been accepted without question in certain departments five years ago, while feeling obliged to accept overseas students with lower qualifications.

2 *Pre-arrival administration*

The investigation of students' perceptions showed that overseas students considered clear, appropriate, well-timed communications to be a vital step in alleviating natural anxieties and clarifying requirements and expectations. The experience of overseas students, from the point of view of staff interviewed, confirmed this need.

There were tremendous differences in perception of pre-arrival administration, according to role, with some staff feeling rather uneasy. The Commonwealth Standing Committee on Student Mobility had emphasized the need for effectively co-ordinated communications, but at present departmental autonomy, lack of resources, and some entrenched administrative procedures seemed to be causing confusion for some potential overseas students.[31]

3 *Arrival procedures*

Evidence from the surveys of students had pointed to the need to feel really welcome and to the strong impact of first impressions. Many staff were conscious of this as they assessed the provisions made and the difficulties. At Loughborough the actual arrival procedure was acknowledged to be 'weak'. At Nottingham, while there was recognition of the need for a combined university meeting service in October to help arriving students, such a service did not then exist. Overseas students were felt likely to suffer disorientation and cultural shock of the most immediate kind, connected with the actual processes of living, and this required tackling forthwith. Many staff saw a pressing need for a basic orientation programme.

4 *Academic provision*

The current situation faced by academic staff was particularly relevant to the question of academic provision for overseas students. Departments were looking for more and more funded research, in line with the universities' requirements and the UGC's priorities. Teaching functions seemed likely to be taken for granted. Staff were left with the feeling that they stood or fell by their research output. Additionally, though, departments were under financial pressure to recruit overseas students – thus producing a problem of conflict, as we saw when considering organizational objectives. Prioritizing research not only seemed to assign a lower status to teaching, it was also at odds with the consequences of a commitment to recruit overseas students, namely an increased teaching load.

The most common observation made by lecturing staff about overseas students was that they represented a greater time commitment than home students. The reasons given included:

- Help needed with English language.
- Lack of the right kind of subject/experimental background, especially in respect of science students.
- Different experiences of learning in their previous educational system, which was most likely to have emphasized fact learning rather than analytical skills, and teacher-led learning rather than self-directed learning.
- Expectations held by overseas students that their tutors would be available for frequent personal consultations.

Interviewees revealed a disjunction between policy planning and policy implementation on how the issue was to be tackled. An increase in the number of overseas students was being sought at the same time as an increasing student load, together with increasing emphasis on research. Jarratt reported that Nottingham, for example, was amongst the ten least favoured of English universities in terms of student–staff ratios in recent years, yet the 1987 Academic Plan showed that many areas of the university were to see a worsening of the student–staff ratio, which would vary from 8 in the School of Medicine to 15 in Arts and some departments of the Faculty of Law and Social Science, by 1989/90.

The Next Steps, published as a result of the Overseas Students Trust survey, found that the standard of teaching of overseas students in these kinds of circumstance left much to be desired.[32]

This aspect of the marketing audit suggested that the institutions were making considerable demands on academics. Research had to be stepped up; tutoring and teaching did not bring promotion; financial economies had to be made, yet overseas student numbers had to be increased and students had to go away qualified and satisfied. Commitment to overseas students by academics in the face of such conflicting demands nevertheless appeared positive in those departments which had a co-ordinated policy. Those members of departments left to fend for themselves, however, varied from the committed to the highly sceptical, thus confirming the need for clear, considered policies to be established within institutions.

5 *Academic support*

Interviewees expressed the view that overseas students needed structured academic support, because many of them were in an academic environment which they could not take for granted. The library facilities, use of computers, handling laboratory or technical equipment, to say nothing of study methods, might all be unfamiliar.

Both academics and policy makers felt that general 'access' courses ought to feature to a greater extent, to familiarize overseas students with their study environment before they embarked upon specific courses or research – a view endorsed by the findings of the CVCP Report on research students[33] which recognized the training role of support staff. For the present, however, academic support areas found themselves providing services for overseas students more or less in parallel with substantive courses.

Home students and European and American students seemed to understand the function of support services and approached the support services with clearly formulated questions or problems; by contrast, other overseas students would sometimes expect support staff to solve more extensive problems and expected a broader range of service. Many support staff stated that the time demands placed on them by some overseas students could therefore be extensive. The various academic support services obviously generated much goodwill towards overseas students despite these extra demands on their time. There was, however, some ambivalence over role. The feeling emerged that although support staff took responsibility for the needs or progress of overseas students in their particular area of expertise, and formed a helping relationship with them, this was not necessarily recognized in the status afforded them.

6 *Language provision*

In expressing his views on the need for universities to ensure that overseas students had sufficient language ability, a head of department encapsulated the views of many staff:

> Language is the paramount problem in connection with overseas students in this department. Even the right paper qualifications still do not ensure that students can understand, discuss or exchange ideas. Those without such qualifications have even more difficulty. This leads to frustration for home students and staff as well as for overseas students themselves. Increasingly stringent checks on language before entry have got to be made.

However, pressures to recruit students created difficulties.

Both universities offered help for overseas students on campus, once they had arrived and either recognized their own problem or were referred for language tuition by members of staff. Although these facilities were available they were not always well used, especially by the students in greatest need. It was considered that in order to develop an effective policy for English language support, tutors needed specific training and equipping with diagnostic tools to bring about an early identification of language problems. Strengthening of liaison between staff and language tutors was urged. An academic in each department with responsibility for the co-ordination of a language policy, but with actual provision outside the department seemed to be preferred. The British Council had found that a 'wedge-shaped' programme which concentrated heavily on language skills in the early days and gradually tapered away, was the best basis for competency;[34] such a programme would require to be fully resourced and funded but might prove cost-effective in the long term.

However, at present, and in common with experiences elsewhere,[35] Loughborough and Nottingham seemed to have an ambivalent approach to the language issue. Both really wanted students to arrive with perfect English, and there was no fully co-ordinated policy for dealing with those who did not.

7   Accommodation

The importance of settled accommodation to the well-being and study potential of overseas students has already been highlighted. Those responsible for accommodation thought complexities in recruitment or admission procedures, produced many accommodation difficulties and that many overseas students came expecting a total package, including finalized accommodation arrangements. Although overseas students were treated in the same way as home students in terms of their accommodation needs, several differences in these needs were identified:

- Vacation accommodation – for halls are generally only open to students during term time and are let to conferences during vacations.
- Special diets and special timing arrangements for meals, especially to meet the needs of Muslims during Ramadan.
- Higher levels of heating during the winter.
- Opportunity to cook their own national foods.
- Difficulty in appreciating the hall philosophy of communality and sharing and the idea of the study–bedroom as a private area used for work as well as living.

Within the existing framework of accommodation provision those at the centre had to maintain a viable system whilst hall wardens and others operating a network of continual contacts with students had to be mindful of their personal welfare needs. It was obvious that recognition of overseas students' material needs had moved forward considerably. The vital importance of personal relationships to project a caring image, remained a key issue.

8   Non-academic and welfare support

Both universities had a range of support facilities available to all students. Despite the view that all students were in need of a variety of support facilities, that the needs of overseas students are essentially no different from those of home students and that they could be provided for by the existing agencies, there were also, however, services through which recognition was given to the special needs of overseas students. At Nottingham there was the Overseas Students Bureau, part of the Students' Union and run largely by second-year overseas students for their fellows; secondly there were the Faculty Advisers for Overseas Students who were members of the academic staff in each faculty (or each department within the faculty in the case of Science and Engineering faculties) and are available to give general advice for overseas students. On both campuses the Student Counselling Services, Chaplaincies, Medical Centres and Students' Unions provided advice and welfare facilities.

However, it has already been observed that many overseas students preferred to have just one referent. They wanted to establish an early one-to-one relationship for both academic and personal support. A number of national agencies such as UKCOSA, the Association of Commonwealth Universities and the National Union of Students, together with all the on-campus support services, were available to tutors when answering queries and giving assistance, but nevertheless a tremendous load and much responsibility could fall upon them when they were already pressed for time. Jenkins has noted that the support and socialization of overseas students in the United States were very well co-ordinated;[36] it was this co-ordination which appeared to be lacking here, despite individual initiatives to offer meaningful liaison.

9 *Social provision*

Many overseas students had imagined that they would socialize with British students and visit the homes of British people during their stay – but even without language problems, they found on arrival that this did not happen.

It is important not to overstate the case, for it was clear that many friendships were made between home and overseas students. However, the barriers to effective social interaction between home and overseas students were increased where overseas students were mature and therefore very different from most home students, or where they were on courses consisting of a large number of overseas students, or where the course they were taking was short and intensive, leaving little time for social activities.

Since increasing numbers of overseas students are mature students taking short, specially designed courses, the lack of contact with home students is bound to continue. Whether this is a problem depends on the expectations and attitudes of the overseas students, but since most come to Britain expecting to get to know British students, many must go home disappointed with this aspect of their social life. For this reason it seems relevant for universities to give consideration to ways of improving the means of social contacts between home and overseas students – for a dissatisfied student is unlikely to recommend his experience to others at home. In the past it had been assumed that social integration was the responsibility of the students and their own affair, but some senior managers are now beginning to accept that the universities should play a part, if not directly in social engineering, at least indirectly in consciousness-raising as far as overseas students are concerned.

Implementation of the marketing system

Even when clear objectives have been set (although, as we have seen, it is debatable whether such objectives can be said to have been set in relation to overseas student recruitment), universities may fail to carry these out effectively. By way of summarizing this analysis of the marketing system, the extent to which it was seen to be successfully implemented at Loughborough and Nottingham is next considered.

The extent to which the universities were planning on an annual basis for overseas student recruitment was difficult to decide. Certainly their Plans set targets for the three years, 1987–90 and the university committees set up to consider recruitment looked at the position on an annual basis. What is less clear is the extent to which this planning encompassed all the areas seen to be so important when staff were assessing the needs of overseas students: areas such as language teaching provision; academic and non-academic support; and accommodation. In any event, departments were seen to be operating with a considerable degree of autonomy when it came to decisions about numbers of overseas students: there did not appear to be the kind of quota system in operation that has been recommended by some.[37] Similarly, there was no explicit policy statement to which staff could turn for guidance on the framing of an effective planning process, either at the central or departmental level. It was apparent from interviews with staff that planning for overseas student recruitment was therefore operating in a piecemeal way. The expressed objective of the universities to recruit as many overseas students as possible *was* being addressed, but the means by which this might be achieved seemed to be limited to the development of promotional materials (information booklets, videos etc.) and the co-ordination of publicity through missions to British Council education fairs abroad and other similar events.

There was no evidence of planning for services to meet overseas students' needs specifically; indeed in some instances senior policy makers stated quite explicitly that overseas students should not be made a special case when it came to service considerations, although as we have seen staff did take account of students' special needs in a variety of ways ranging from teaching provision to their treatment in hall.

Just as organizations need to plan for the implementation of objectives, so they must control to ensure that the goals being set are achieved. Once again, this presupposes that managers are in agreement as to the goals. The generally agreed goal was that of increasing overseas student numbers: the check on how effectively this was being achieved was an annual appraisal of student numbers. As the sub-goals that would aid the recruitment of overseas students were not generally agreed there were no controls on the effectiveness of such aspects of provision for overseas students as the efficiency of accommodation provision, how satisfactorily language teaching was being received, and the operation of counselling and support services.

One of the clearest findings to emerge from the survey of staff was the lack of a coherent communication system with regard to overseas student recruitment and the management of overseas students on the campus. The function that appeared to cause most difficulty in this regard was accommodation provision. Not knowing how many students were likely to arrive on the first day of the academic year could result in chaos for some students, as well of course for the hapless staff who had to deal with them. Instances of confusion over information mailed to or received by students compounded the problems. More broadly, there was no overall policy on the kinds of information *needed* for the successful implementation of a marketing programme. As with other aspects of implementation the management information systems were piecemeal. Those in operation, particularly those systems run by individual departments, could be extremely effective: departmental administrative assistants were often the source of clear, thorough and timely information about individuals and groups of students. University-wide systems to match this type of individual recall had not however been developed.

The Marketing Activity Review

Having established the problems posed by the environment in which universities are operating and discussed the perceived needs of overseas students and the responses of the universities through an appraisal of their marketing systems, those marketing activities that should be pursued to help meet the objective of recruiting more overseas students will now be considered. In addition, the question of how far universities *should* be pursuing this objective will be addressed.

A critical approach to the four P's of marketing (product, price, place, promotion) was especially helpful in analysing the marketing activities of the universities. The alternative of a 'marketing matrix', in which the four P's are 'dumped' in favour of three 'marketer elements': offering, price and communication, together with 'customer elements', provided a more relevant structure. The customer elements have already been assessed in the Marketing Audit, above. The 'offering' is considered under the headings 'Courses and research programmes' and 'Support services'; 'price' is analysed under 'Fees and costs'; 'communication' under 'Promotion'. While there are clear similarities with more conventional attitudes to marketing in this approach, there is a much greater emphasis on the 'synergistic whole' of offering, price and communication strategies which enables much clearer consideration of the special nature of higher education.[38] It was evident from the interviews with staff that it was precisely this overall concept of strategy formulation that appeared to be lacking; the Marketing Activity Review is therefore a means of addressing this problem.

Courses and research programmes

The teaching content of the offering is of great importance to students – an argument to be developed in Chapter 2. From the student surveys it was found that students were on the whole generally satisfied with the courses offered and with the teaching and research supervision they received. These offerings have several important features in common:

- they have evolved to meet a clear, well-researched need in an effectively segmented area of the market,

- they have a vocational orientation,
- there is a high level of staff commitment to the development of the courses in line with market demands.

Loughborough University's Department of Civil Engineering WEDC course; the Department of Library and Information Studies masters' courses in Library and Information Studies; the Department of Electronics and Electrical Engineering's courses; the Department of PE and Sports Science courses, are some examples of the strengths of the university's product offering. Nottingham University's School of Education B.Ed. for Hong Kong students; the diploma courses in Insurance Studies and Insurance Management of the Department of Industrial Economics, Accountancy and Insurance; the courses offered by the Department of Agriculture at Sutton Bonington, are similarly strongly targeted at overseas students.

There are undoubtedly ways in which universities might improve on the content and teaching of courses: Fransson's description of an 'internationalized' university system might offer some stimulating ideas.[39] There is, quite naturally, a British bias to the teaching and content of courses that can at times leave overseas students feeling excluded and alien. On the other hand, many students come here precisely because they want a high quality *British* education that will be respected back home. Any internationalizing of teaching programmes should therefore not detract from this high quality offering.

One further measure to indicate the effectiveness of the offering, apart from students' expressions of general satisfaction with courses, is the success of overseas students compared with their UK counterparts. There was some assumption by staff that because of the problems of language overseas students had a consistently higher failure rate than British students. However, on examining failure and withdrawal rates for 1982, 1985 and 1986 (two sample years and the year immediately preceding the investigation), it was clear that the pass, fail and drop-out rates for overseas students were not very different from those for home students. The proportion of overseas students who received first or upper second class degrees was however considerably less than for home students.

It seemed, therefore, that the perceptions of university staff, regarding success rates, may have been based on their encounters with specific overseas students rather than on the actual qualifications achieved by students as a whole. Alternatively, students' poor standard of English may have misled observers into thinking that certain students would not be successful. Some staff interviewed thought it a possibility that, as long as meaning was not lost, examiners were prepared to accept a less fluent standard of English if the writing style suggested that they were marking the work of overseas students. This would lead to more overseas students being successful than staff might have anticipated.

Several staff had also mentioned the high emotional and financial costs of failure for overseas students. Faced with such anguish some academics had felt a particular obligation to aid struggling students. Despite this variety of staff impressions, in the event, overseas students were not significantly more likely to fail or withdraw than their British counterparts.

Nevertheless, despite the evidence of these examination and withdrawal figures, need for continuing vigilance over standards and the performance of overseas students is recognized. The CVCP Report on *Academic Standards in Universities* stressed the importance of maintaining comparability across universities.[40] Just as important is the perception by both home and overseas students (and their sponsors and future employers) that all students are being assessed in the same way. The concern at Loughborough and Nottingham was not so much that standards were threatened but much more that staff were faced with greater problems in teaching overseas students with poor English. Greater expenditure of time and effort on overseas students was the issue raised by staff most often, not that of standards.

Support services

While students expressed general satisfaction at the course content, teaching and supervision they received, the same cannot be said of the various kinds of support services provided. One of the most significant findings of the investigation was that overseas students do not perceive the product offering solely in terms of the academic qualification they will gain: these support services were a central preoccupation, especially if things were not organized smoothly. For students, the product offering included the whole range of support services available to them.

Accommodation was especially important to students. They had largely expected this to be arranged alongside their tuition as a package deal, despite both universities' clear statements to the contrary in information sent out with offers of places. The universities had, however, encountered problems in the administration of accommodation allocation to overseas students for a variety of other reasons. Lack of clear management information had caused uncertainty as to the numbers of students arriving; students bringing their families, despite advice that married accommodation was not available caused problems; overseas students' special needs of diet, religious observance, relationships with other nationalities and unfamiliarity with British culture, meant a great deal more support from accommodation officers was required than for home students. It was apparent therefore that the co-ordination of recruitment on to courses and the most basic of support services, accommodation, was poor. The strength of feeling engendered amongst students should serve as an indication that this situation must be remedied if the offering is to meet students' expectations.

The other principal support that students – and academic staff – saw as crucial to the successful completion of study, as well as enabling students to benefit from their time in the UK, was language tuition. As we saw, despite the language qualifications demanded of students, many came to Britain with inadequate English for undertaking advanced study. There is obviously a case for making a pre-sessional course compulsory for overseas students and including the cost in a complete tuition package.

Ongoing weekly language classes were also provided, but the efficacy of these was limited. The British Council model of ensuring its students reach a minimum standard before arrival at university through attendance at language schools elsewhere in the UK; urging students to attend a pre-sessional course and through its English Language Co-ordination Unit paying for students to have up to four hours a week tuition when necessary, is one that universities could well emulate. The emphasis in this approach is once again on seeing language support as an intrinsic element in the product offering, rather than as a dispensable extra.

The general pastoral support given to overseas students was largely co-ordinated through the Student Counselling Services or the Overseas Students' Bureau at Nottingham. On both campuses counsellors considered that their 'problem'-oriented image might actually detract from their usefulness as a general advice agency, and this perception was borne out from students' comments. Students could also use the Students' Union for general advice, and they frequently did so. However, it was clear from interviews with both students and staff that the first line of defence for most students was their academic tutor in the department. Students, in the absence of a clear organization designed to meet their pastoral needs, made considerable demands on academic staff for all kinds of personal support. Staff recognized the importance of their roles as personal as well as academic tutors, but inevitably in the present climate these demands place an extra burden on them. The suggestion by a senior counsellor and others that a university-run Overseas Students Bureau should be established, to co-ordinate practical and pastoral support activities for overseas students, seemed sensible. The University of Kent has an office with special responsibility for such activities, with an overseas students officer, in addition to the normal tutorial and counselling services.[41]

The academic support given by non-academic departments was also seen to play a significant role in students' perceptions of the product offering. The university library was important for all students. The computer centres also recognized that foreign students had special needs; they in their turn made specific demands on staff. The sensitivity with which these often unwarranted expectations were dealt with was a marked feature of these support services, as indeed with other forms of academic support across the campuses. Students received considerable help and support from technicians, and this relationship was one that again proved to be an important element in the product offering. Deciding how far to go in supporting students called for good interpersonal skills on the part of support staff. The relationships struck between the whole range of technical, administrative and domestic staff and overseas students were an additional factor in student perceptions of the universities. Again and again in the data from questionnaires and interviews of students the significance was evident of this network of relationships for students' feelings about the value they were receiving.

In discussions with individual members of staff their interest in and commitment to caring for students was often very marked; however, they were perhaps unaware of their importance in the scheme of things. A staff training pro- gramme which would address the issues of overseas students' welfare across *all* university functions could be one means of heightening such awareness. At present the universities' training programmes concentrate largely on academic and senior administrative staff; staff training across all functions would appear to be essential for the effective implementation of marketing activities and especially as a way of emphasizing the particular needs of overseas students.

It was apparent from the literature that planning the offering across the board, and including support services of various kinds within the package offered to students, were issues that had to be addressed by managements if unversities are to compete successfully in the market-place. In its report on *Fair Practices in Higher Education* in the USA the Carnegie Council emphasized the importance of effective support services and produced recommendations to encourage a mutual awareness between colleges and students of their rights and responsibilities. Specifically, students were recommended to ask 'What support services does this institution offer?' (Examples would include counselling, health care, compensatory education, and job placement.[42]) The failure of institutions to consider these needs was instanced by the Assistant Director of Admissions at Southern Illinois University. He cited the case of one college that admitted foreign students without planning for adequate language support. The students also became upset at the living arrangements at the college. 'They did not like the American food they were required to eat and did not like living with American room mates . . . the students decided to quit college and return to their home country. What could have been a rich educational experience for the students, the college and the town ended in disaster.'[43] It was emphasized in another study that 'Support services in the foreign student adviser's office must be adequate to provide the services required by these students' and that administrators at all levels should 'carefully study, analyze and plan all details of the foreign student program before the foreign students appear on campus'.[44] Further, the point has been made that this concern to ensure services are adequate before students are recruited is sensible in terms of future recruitment, reinforcing the findings of this investigation. 'One of the most effective ways to lower the cost of student recruitment is to improve student satisfaction on campus. It is axiomatic that satisfied students are the college's best advertisers.'[45]

This American experience has been supported in the UK literature. The Overseas Students Trust survey found that institutions needed to reinforce their pastoral care arrangements,[46] while the AUT/UKCOSA Conference on Responsible Recruitment came out unequivocally in favour of establishing effective support services, together with staff training programmes, as part of a co-ordinated approach to student recruitment.[47]

Fees and costs

Pitching the fee levels for overseas students from non-EC countries has become a major concern for UK universities since the adoption of the full-cost fees policy in 1980. While the Jarratt Report recommended overseas students as a useful source of revenue it was also cautious: institutions should be careful that they *did* cover the costs of overseas students to the institution. And herein lies the problem for universities: on the one hand they are exhorted by government to increase their revenue through overseas student recruitment, while on the other they must ensure that fees are sufficiently buoyant to cover the extra costs incurred. In setting fee levels each year universities undertake no detailed costing of students' variable use of services, nor on the cost of administering overseas student recruitment, as a means of assessing realistic fees. Pricing is very much related to fees charged elsewhere and the perception that keeping the cost to the student down as far as possible will enhance recruitment.

There are problems with this approach. Most seriously for universities is the failure to acknowledge the real cost to institutions of recruiting overseas students. From interviews with staff it was apparent that overseas students were making tremendous time and effort demands on already overstretched academics who are being pressured to bring research money in and push publications out. Financial incentives to departments for numbers of overseas students recruited were not passed on to those staff dealing with them, which created further resentment. As we have seen, support services were similarly being stretched by the demands of overseas students, who took up a dispro-portionate amount of expertise, time and resources. We have also seen that the failure of universities to develop these services would probably have an adverse effect on future recruitment: Catch 22. Once again, experience in the USA confirmed that British universities might be misguided in assuming that 'full-cost' fees could solve resourcing problems – especially when those costs had not been accurately assessed. Foreign students *were* seen as an asset to institutions, but only if institutions approach enrolment 'responsibly, sensibly and efficiently'. Some of the costs which were detailed, to be considered and built in to the fee structure were:

- membership of relevant organizations (such as UKCOSA in the case of British institutions)
- production and postage of information materials
- the cost of travel overseas for staff promotion exercises[48]

To these relatively minor items of expenditure should be added an estimate of the additional time demands on staff and the provision of the support services detailed above.

At present, universities have generally not come to grips with this kind of qualitative costing. The Performance Indicators Steering Committee in its identification of 39 indicators was particularly concerned with input, process and output from a quantitative perspective. The impact of one set of indicators on another because of, for example, the overemphasis on one set of activities to the detriment of others, is difficult to assess in this kind of model. The impact of overseas student recruitment on staff performance in other areas is not quantifiable by means of this type of audit. Nor is it possible to assess the likely cost of offering a particular service to an overseas student compared with a home student.[49] The FTE is blind to such distinctions.

To summarize this consideration of fees and costs it would seem appropriate to propose that universities undertake such a costing exercise. A major objective at the moment is to concentrate considerable effort on overseas student recruitment, but there appears to be little evidence that this is necessarily a cost-effective exercise in the long term. In any event, as we have noted, if such recruitment is to be effective more resources will be required for the development of support services. This too needs to be costed. On the other hand the benefits to universities, other than possible short-term revenue gains, should also be estimated. Long-term goals and immediate objectives would then require further consideration in the light of these additional data.

Promotion

From the evidence of the interviews with staff, it was clear that communication was particularly relevant to the management of overseas recruitment. Communication to existing students, communications across campuses and communication with the market were all of considerable importance. The most successful of the marketing activities undertaken by both Loughborough and Nottingham appeared to be that of communicating with the market – promoting the universities to prospective students. Communication more generally was rather less well implemented.

Even with promotion, there were problems, however. Students had reported difficulties in receiving pre-course information and in communicating with the universities – difficulties which had been acknowledged by administrators. The kind of information sent out to prospective students was also criticized by some staff: there were some fears of 'hype' and a failure to offer students a realistic picture of life at a British university, warts and all.

Central university committees at Loughborough and Nottingham have co-ordinated efforts to improve promotion. Nevertheless, care still needs to be exercised on communications with students. Producing the material is only one aspect of the problem: ensuring that these materials, as well as clear and timely information, actually reach prospective students is essential for promotion to be effective.

Advertising through satisfied returning students is also obviously a most helpful form of promotion, and again, this requires further attention. While visits by staff overseas are helpful, the longer-term benefits of students spreading the word amongst their compatriots cannot be overestimated. Past students comprise a network of contacts worldwide that could be further tapped by universities.

While promotion to the market was being effectively developed, there was little evidence that the importance of communication systems on campus for the management of the recruitment process was being similarly recognized. In the student and staff surveys this was a recurrent problem. Students were especially critical of the lack of information on accommodation, both immediately pre-arrival and on arrival. Staff too were critical of this area, as we have already noted. Communication was similarly a problem for staff in other functional areas. It could be difficult on occasion to gather the whole story about a student with problems; communication between staff in pastoral and academic roles was seen to be important to remedy this. While this is true for all students, the problems may cause much more distress to overseas students and encompass worries about accommodation, immigration requirements, language difficulties, cultural adjustment, and concern for a family left at home. The establishment of a university rather than largely student-run Overseas Students' Bureau was seen to be one means of co-ordinating advice and counselling facilities for students, and also as a centre to which hard-pressed academic tutors could refer their students.

The marketing activities being implemented by both universities were therefore very variable in quality. It was evident from the student and staff surveys that there was a mismatch between student expectation and university performance across the activities discussed above. In particular, support services of various kinds were perceived as requiring further resources to meet these expectations. However, there was a considerable difficulty in that overseas students are recruited to balance the books; further resourcing of services to meet their needs must therefore be viable. The whole question of whether or not universities should be recruiting so keenly in the overseas market if there are only short-term revenue gains rather than long-term profitability should be addressed.

Conclusion

Marketing and managing the recruitment of overseas students: recommendations

1. There is an urgent need to provide accurate figures of the likely cost to universities of overseas student recruitment. This study has shown that the notion of overseas students being only a 'marginal cost' to institutions could be mistaken. Support services, staff time, technical support, and accommodation, are all areas likely to be heavily used by overseas students. The objective expressed in universities' Plans of recruiting heavily in the overseas market on revenue considerations alone may well require reconsideration. On the other hand institutions may well decide there are other equally valid educational and cultural reasons for continuing such recruitment. It would appear to be essential, however, that strategic decisions should be based on the fullest possible management information. At the moment this appears to

be lacking. An investigation of the cost of recruitment would therefore enable a debate to be mounted within institutions on the objectives of recruiting overseas students on a more rational basis than at present.

2. A clear policy statement on overseas student recruitment should be developed by each institution as a result of this debate and coherent cross-campus strategies implemented.

3. Admissions policies should be co-ordinated across departments, with clear guidelines on English language qualifications and waivers only in wholly exceptional circumstances. The implementation of admissions policies should be carefully monitored.

4. Further consideration should be given as a result of the findings of this research to the importance of various kinds of support for overseas students. Course design should be accompanied by service design across accommodation; academic and non-academic support; welfare and social provision.

5. Staff training programmes should be organized to include all functions and grades of staff dealing with overseas students. It was clear that there were special demands made on staff dealing with students from different cultures and that staff training would be helpful to improve the level of awareness of students' special needs. Liaison with other agencies – UKCOSA, the British Council, the Overseas Students Trust and the National Union of Students – would also be helpful in framing training programmes and fostering further co-operative links.

6. There is a need to monitor student satisfaction. The results of the student survey highlighted a mismatch between student expectations and universities' performance; this should serve to emphasize the importance of continuing control of marketing activities by management. A survey of students should therefore form part of an overall marketing strategy and be conducted annually.

7. Communications were often see to be inefficient. Universities should conduct communications audits to enable more effective systems to be developed. A strategy for recruiting overseas students should address this issue as a matter of urgency. To date only the promotion of courses to the market appeared to have been considered important. The investigation of Loughborough and Nottingham universities indicated, however, that communication channels within universities were equally important in ensuring that staff understood policy and its implications for their roles and that services were properly co-ordinated.

8. Finally, perhaps the most important point of all is that universities should be adopting a strategic approach to their marketing activities. At present, the need to react with urgency to pressing immediate problems has overwhelmed many institutions: a longer view has been neglected in favour of short-term expediency. Only when pro-active strategies are developed by universities though, rather than re-active tactics, can they claim to be managing effectively for a long-term future.

References

1. Committee of Vice-Chancellors and Principals, *Report of the Steering Committee for Efficiency Studies in Universities*, London, Committee of Vice-Chancellors and Principals, 1985, (The Jarratt Report), p. 16.
2. Ibid.
3. P. Kotler, *Marketing for Non-profit Organizations*, Englewood Cliffs, NJ, Prentice-Hall, 1975, *passim*.
4. Ibid, pp. 56–74.
5. M. Kinnell, 'International marketing in UK higher education: some issues in relation to marketing educational programmes to overseas students', *European Journal of Marketing*, 23(5), 7–21, 1989.
   C. H. Lovelock and M. L. Rothschild, 'Uses, abuses and misuses of marketing in higher education', in *Marketing in College Admissions: a Broadening of Perspectives*, New York, College Entrance Examination Board, 1980, pp. 31–69.
6. S. Majaro, *International Marketing: a Strategic Approach to World Markets*, London, Allen & Unwin, 1977, p. 31.
7. P. Kotler, *Marketing for Non-profit Organizations*, pp. 163–4.
8. C. H. Lovelock, 'Theoretical contributions from services and non-business marketing', in O. C. Ferrell, S. W. Brown and C. W. Lamb, *Conceptual and Theoretical Developments in Marketing*, Chicago, American Marketing Association, 1979.
9. J. Carswell, *Government and the Universities in Britain: Programme and Performance*, Cambridge, Cambridge University Press, 1985.
10. Loughborough University of Technology, *The Academic Plan to 1990: the First Phase of a Longer Term Strategy*, Loughborough, Loughborough University of Technology, 1987, p. 7.
11. J. Armenio, 'Back to the Agora: marketing foreign admissions', *Journal of the National Association of College Admissions Counsellors*, 22 (1978), 30–34.
12. S. Beltz, 'For all matters concerning overseas students', *Association of Commonwealth Universities Bulletin of Current Documentation*, 75 (1986), 16–17.
13. S. Shotnes, *International Comparisons in Overseas Student Affairs*, London, United Kingdom Council on Overseas Student Affairs, 1986.
14. P. Kotler, *Marketing for Non-profit Organizations*, pp. 18–19.
15. G. Williams, M. Woodhall and V. O'Brien, *Overseas Students and their Place of Study: Report of a Survey*, London, Overseas Students Trust, 1986.
16. S. Stone, 'Developing a marketing strategy', *Coombe Lodge Report*, 17 (1985), 679–84.
17. L. Litten, 'Marketing higher education. Benefits and risks for the American academic system', *Journal of Higher Education*, 51 (1980), 40–59.
18. G. Williams, M. Woodhall and V. O'Brien, *Overseas Students and their Place of Study: Report of a Survey*.
19. P. Kotler, 'Applying marketing theory to college admissions', in *A Role for Marketing in College Admissions. Proceedings of the Colloquium on College Admissions, Fontana, Wisconsin. May 16–18, 1976*, New York, College Entrance Examination Board, 1976, pp. 54–72.
20. British Council, *Higher Education Market Survey. Jordan*, London, British Council, 1985, p. 15.
21. British Council, *Higher Education Market Survey. Thailand*, London, British Council, 1986, p. 21.
22. Ibid.
23. British Council, *Higher Education Market Survey. Singapore*, London, British Council, 1985, p. 20.

24. P. Kotler, *Marketing for Non-profit Organizations*, p. 61.
25. J. Armenio, 'Back to the Agora: marketing foreign admissions'.
26. R. Cowell, 'Education gets the soap-powder treatment', *Times Higher Education Supplement*, 4 June 1982, 13.
27. L. Litten, 'Marketing higher education: benefits and risks for the American academic system'.
28. M. Mackey, 'The selling of the sheepskin', *Change* 12 (1980), 28–33.
29. S. Shotnes (ed.), *International Comparisons in Overseas Student Affairs*, London, UKCOSA, 1986.
30. O. Kleinberg and W. Hull, *At a Foreign University. An International Study of Adaptation and Coping*, New York, Praeger, 1979.
31. Commonwealth Standing Committee on Student Mobility, *Fifth Report. Commonwealth Student Mobility: Commitment and Resources*, London, Commonwealth Secretariat, 1986.
32. Sir K. Berrill, *The Next Steps. Overseas Student Policy into the 1990s*. London, Overseas Students Trust, 1987.
33. Committee of Vice-Chancellors and Principals, *Postgraduate Training and Research*, London, CVCP, 1985.
34. British Council, *Study Modes and Academic Development of Overseas Students*, London, British Council, 1980.
35. G. Geoghegan, *Non-native Speakers of English at Cambridge University*, Cambridge, Bell Education Trust, 1983.
36. H. M. Jenkins, *Educating Students from Other Nations*, San Francisco, Jossey-Bass, 1983.
37. S. Shotnes (ed.), *International Comparisons in Overseas Student Affairs*, pp. 76–7.
38. C. H. Lovelock, 'Theoretical contributions from service and non-business marketing'.
39. L. Fransson, 'Internationalizing the universities', in *Proceedings of the 25th Anniversary AIR Forum, Promoting Excellence through Information and Technology. Portland, Oregon, April 28–May 1, 1985*. Portland, Oregon, Association for Institutional Research, 1985.
40. Committee of Vice-Chancellors and Principals, *Academic Standards in Universities*, London, CVCP, 1986, p. 5.
41. Association of University Teachers and United Kingdom Council for Overseas Student Affairs, *Responsible Recruitment: Report of a Conference, Feb. 20 1986*. London, AUT/UKCOSA, 1986, p. 9.
42. Carnegie Council on Policy Studies in Higher Education, *Fair Practices in Higher Education*, San Francisco, Jossey-Bass, 1979, pp. 53–74.
43. R. E. Thomas, 'So you want to recruit foreign students?', *Journal of the National Association of College Admissions Counsellors*, 19 (1974), 11–12.
44. T. E. Sharp, 'Institutional administration and the foreign student program', *College and University* 57 (1982), 323–6.
45. P. Kotler, 'Applying marketing theory to college admissions'.
46. G. Williams, M. Woodhall and V. O'Brien, *Overseas Students and their Place of Study*.
47. Association of University Teachers and United Kingdom Council for Overseas Student Affairs, *Responsible Recruitment*.
48. K. Rogers, 'Foreign students: economic benefit or liability?', *College Board Review*, 133 (1984), 20–25.
49. Performance Indicator Steering Committee, *University Management Information and Performance Indicator Statistics*, London, CVCP, 1987.

2
Teaching and Learning

Barry Elsey

At the heart of university education provision for overseas students should be the goal of effective teaching and learning. Overseas students have a pressing need, perhaps above all else, to return home with the inner satisfaction and the outward measure of successful academic achievement. Of course, other features of university and British life are valuable too, such as decent living accommodation and welfare services, good sporting and cultural facilities and experience of the British people and society. But these are generally of lesser meaning and value than academic achievement, a finding that emerged clearly from the students' responses in questionnaires and interviews.

This need is generally understood by the marketeers of university education. At the same time achieving effective teaching and learning constitutes the main problem. It is increasingly recognized that university teachers need training and development in the skills of effective teaching and student learning, for no longer is it sufficient to expound knowledge without good enabling processes of learning. Similarly, students from home or overseas need help in fostering the skills of effective learning. Previous education is only partly a preparation for the academic demands, or better still, the requirements to think and learn critically and independently, that comprise the essence of a good university education.

This chapter explores these issues and relates them to the survey findings of the teaching and learning experiences of the overseas students at both Loughborough and Nottingham universities. The chapter concludes on a practical note about future needs for change by institutions to render teaching and learning for overseas students more effective. The emphasis is on the context within which students learn; more specific reference to one vital aspect – the tutor–student relationship – is made in Chapter 3.

It should be apparent that there is an implicit statement of value running through this chapter, noted by the frequent reference to the idea of effectiveness in teaching and learning. Behind that practical value – which few would dispute as an objective, only perhaps argue about how effective teaching and learning are to be achieved – lies the belief that it is both a matter of professional pride and marketing integrity that university education for overseas students must be a high-value experience. A great deal of money has changed hands and many overseas students have placed themselves in a high-risk position, with the fear of failure looming large in most minds. Overseas students have a compelling need to succeed academically and the university has a moral duty to teach effectively and enable them to learn effectively. News of failure or even dissatisfaction travels fast and the overseas student recruitment policy is soon at risk. But more importantly, ineffective teaching and learning betray the ideals of university education, which is the pursuit of excellence through the development of knowledge and critical thinking.

It is not so common to hear the desirability of effective teaching and learning expounded intra-murally, except, perhaps, where universities have established staff development units. It is more often the case that the values and practices of effective teaching and learning are expressed strongly in university departments of adult and continuing education, the formerly named extra-mural providers for the general public. University adult continuing education, which might reasonably include in-service teacher education and other professional develop-ment provision, is as much interested in the processes of learning as in the knowledge content of academic subjects. The simple idea is that teaching and learning go naturally together, but that it is also necessary to ensure that they do so by an equal concern with how teaching is conducted as with what is taught.

The time-honoured practice is to emphasize the value of informed discussion, the lubricant of democratic citizenship through knowledge discourse. In con-temporary times the forward-thinking adult educators practise a wider range of teaching and learning approaches. At the apex is the adult learner and in recent years much attention has been devoted to enabling adults to learn effectively. Emphasis is still placed on active learning through discussion, but there is now more concern with the skills of self-directed learning and with techniques of explaining, as well as improvements to the communication of ideas through lectures, seminars, demonstrations and the use of educational technology.

These ideas and practices have not been lost on intra-mural university teaching and learning, of course, but are rather slower to take hold. Perhaps in general intra-mural staff have been more concerned with research and publi-cation, possibly also the time-consuming business of university politics and administration, to pay much attention to teaching and learning. As explained earlier, though, this attitude is no longer justifiable and more of a service mentality towards overseas students is required.

It is useful at this juncture to make explicit the meaning of effective teaching and learning. From there it is also worthwhile establishing some basic principles of adult teaching and learning, on the assumption that most overseas students are often of mature age and have experience of adult roles and responsibilities. In some respects this is not altogether fair on intra-mural university education, particularly at undergraduate level, for the majority of students are not really of mature years. Moreover there is a deliberate use of adult education yardsticks to judge intra-mural approaches to teaching and learning. None the less there is value in explicitly stating those teaching and learning goals that are commanding a growing support, in practice as well as rhetoric.

A very clear statement on effective teaching comes from a recent book by Brown and Atkins, which is worth quoting in full:

> Effective teaching is intellectually demanding in that it requires the teacher to know, in a deep sense, the subject being taught. To teach effectively you need to be able to think and problem-solve, to analyse a topic, to reflect upon what is an appropriate approach, to select key strategies and materials, and to organize and structure ideas, information, and tasks for students. None of these activities occurs in a vacuum. Effective teaching is socially challenging in that it takes place in the context of a department and institution which may have unexamined traditions and conflicting goals and values. Most important of all, effective teaching requires the teacher to consider what the students know, to communicate clearly to them, and to stimulate them to learn, think, communicate, and perhaps in their turn, to stimulate their teachers.[1]

This undoubtedly underlines the point that effective teaching is as much about excellence as research and publication, and is worthy of the same effort.

With regard to effective learning it is clear that this stems in part from good teaching. In adult education it is commonplace to argue that the students have to take proper responsibility for their own learning. The role of the teacher is to facilitate effective adult learning. Effectiveness from a learner's perspective is measured by degrees and other awards of academic achievement. This is emphatically the case with overseas students, with the added bonus, hopefully, of increased self-confidence and the power to express ideas critically as well as clearly, often in another language.

At the core of a progressive approach to teaching and learning in university education is the attempt to make both more effective, and even consumer- or user-friendly, by systematizing the former and reappraising the needs for the latter. In extreme form the traditional university approach embodies undemocratic and unadult practices. It starts from the premise that teachers are the dominant force in communicating knowledge and that learning is more passive than active. Teacher knows best, and this is embodied in the curriculum, over which the learner has very little say. The progressive approach is learner-centred and attempts to involve the adult learner more fully in taking control over their own learning. Emphasis is placed on experiential learning, that is, a systematic attempt to bring learning together into one process; where concrete experiences lead to reflection and abstract, conceptual thought before 'real life' application. This comes closer to natural processes of learning and is made real by encouraging the practices of group discussion, active and critical questioning, negotiated and contract-based, self-directed learning within the disciplined framework of academic education. These are challenging ideas in university education generally and are just as applicable to home as to overseas students. Certainly they pose problems for both kinds of students for it is still not widespread practice in school education to foster the ideas of student-centred, progressive learning, especially at the interface with higher education or employment.

After this bold and somewhat provocative overture it is necessary to approach the subject in more measured tones. The rest of this chapter, then, proceeds from the teaching and learning experiences of the overseas students to that of the attitudes and perceptions of university academic staff, which is then placed in context by referring to relevant aspects of university life, particularly the structure of roles and underpinning professional values which are currently being stretched and strained to the point of tension and conflict.

The final part of the chapter deals with the question of meeting the needs of both parties to teaching and learning in university education and catching the wind of change that is leading to new ideas and approaches.

It is not considered necessary here to dwell on the fine-print details of the research methodology or sample sizes and specific findings from the various surveys and interviews with overseas students and academic staff. An outline of research methods can be found above in the Introduction. Instead, attention is focused on the highlights of the research where it relates to teaching and learning and the wider context of change, as well as conservatism, that surrounds the policy and practice of energetically recruiting overseas students. It is important to note, though, that the research did have a problem and issues focus, which is perhaps inevitable in a project of such human interest. But this is balanced with the practice of seeking information on likes as well as dislikes, successes as much as failures. A pertinent example is that several overseas students looking back on their learning experiences, both academic and general, were at pains to point out that they had overcome their problems and difficulties which were mostly experienced at the beginning of their time at university. There was little evidence of an abiding anger or bitterness, of being cheated or treated badly by people or the 'system'. At the same time this is no cause for complacency, for the problems and issues were real at the time.

Allowing for the previous remark about sample details it is useful to broadly describe the overseas students as comprising a variety of types and backgrounds. Overseas students, expressed in the simplest terms, are a heterogeneous group as shown in Table 2.1. The response by male and female students

Table 2.1 Surveys of overseas students in final year of study at both universities

Country group	Loughborough University Sample Completed		Nottingham University Sample Completed	
	Size (N)	Questionnaires (%)	Size (N)	Questionnaires (%)
Far East and Antipodes	120	20(17%)	101	58(57%)
Europe	38	7(18%)	35	10(29%)
Americas	12	2(17%)	31	9(29%)
Africa	94	21(22%)	20	15(75%)
Middle East	88	10(11%)	17	5(29%)
Not known	2	1(50%)	—	—
	354	61(17%)	204	97(48%)

was roughly in proportion to their overall numbers as was the undergraduate/ postgraduate and research student response.

The really important point to note is that the geographical areas producing most fee payers have little Western tradition of education and this in turn has implications for language competency and familiarization with typical modes of study in universities. Many of these countries can now cope with their own nationals at first-degree level, so recruitment is increasingly aimed at those looking for shorter and more specialized higher-degree courses. In some respects, also, a first degree at an overseas university (i.e. the UK, USA, etc.) is rather a second choice or 'overspill' circumstance.

Cultural affinities also tend to be few, which creates a strain on the simple notion that overseas students should be expected to 'fit in' to the British university system and not have their own expectations and needs. Clearly the days of the grateful overseas students coming to the former 'mother country' for some post-colonial higher education is mistaken. Instead it is more realistic to expect rightfully demanding consumers of a service for which there is increasing choice elsewhere. As argued in Chapter 1, a marketing orientation is essential for universities in today's circumstances.

Against that general background it is appropriate to describe the relevant findings from the reflections of those in their final year of study. Unless it is really significant no distinction will be made between the findings from the two universities and this practice will apply throughout the remainder of the chapter.

From the pilot survey overseas students undertaking a variety of courses identified a number of needs and problems concerned with teaching and learning. Some felt a need for a compulsory orientation course on reading, writing and study skills. The desirability of lecturers supplying detailed hand-outs was also emphasized, as was the need to speak more clearly and reduce the quirks of English accents and expressions. Some expressed a need for help with their own spoken and written English through language classes.

The nature of the relationship between academic tutor and student, as highlighted in Chapter 3, was clearly seen as of pivotal importance and the recurring theme of regarding the tutor as 'guide, philosopher and friend' was first voiced through the pilot survey. There was undoubtedly an expectation that the individual tutorial would somehow meet needs and would be echoed by a sensitive and caring tutor. Of more particular note, the need to have the British approach to learning and education explained was identified; so too were the mysteries of academic assessment.

In the subsequent survey proper teaching and learning aspects of overseas students' experiences were obtained through like/dislike questions and in the data processing further refinements dealt with problems that they seemed to share with home students, as well as those of a special kind. Out of this the principal needs were summarized.

Of the aspects of university education they liked, overseas students empha-sized the importance attached to having an opportunity to improve professional performance, enhance career prospects, and update specialist knowledge. The idea of education as an instrument or means to other things was reinforced through an acknowledgement of the relevance and practical applicability of most courses.

On the dislike side, criticism was made about the lack of personal attention and a proper sense of professional responsibility amongst some academic staff. In particular the absence of constructive feedback on much laboured work was keenly felt by some. This had considerable relevance for our detailed consideration of the relationship between tutors and students.

Others complained that there was no mechanism for ensuring that overseas students really could cope with the academic work before they arrived, so that thereafter they could proceed with confidence. This problem was to a large extent overcome where bridging courses were in operation, as in the case of Hong Kong students on courses leading to the B.Ed. degree.

A general understanding of the problems of home students in the teaching and learning sphere provided the basis for speculating which of those things might be shared with overseas students. These revolved around limited facilities, notably in library and computer services, especially where the expansion of student numbers had created intense pressure on the availability of the tools of learning.

With regard to teaching and learning in the classroom or lecture-hall context, both home and overseas students suffered under boring and inadequately prepared lectures. Another shared difficulty was experienced wherever the educational approach of the lecturer or department was not explained but deemed to be self-evident, more often discovered painfully and slowly. Criticism of the written examination as the sole method of assessment was also a shared concern.

Overseas students acutely felt the limited personal attention and guidance given by academic staff, a lack of study skills courses and the almost complete absence of anything other than an ethnocentric British view in some areas of study.

On the basis of the survey of final-year overseas students, which had a representative flavour, their principal needs were for good quality rapport with their academic tutors, especially for a sympathetic listening ear and personal support in what was for many a difficult learning experience. Academically the need for good quality feedback on written work and other performance-based learning activity was keenly felt and strongly expressed. Related to this was the need for a more responsive course organization which paid more than lip-service to the strengths and weaknesses of overseas students and their individuality. This pointed the way to more student-centred learning with a higher level of personal interaction with academic tutors. Not surprisingly, overseas students were also very aware of their language difficulties and their need for practical help with written and spoken English.

The research team quite appreciated that retrospective summaries by overseas students had a limitation, in so far as there was a tendency to gloss over their initial experiences and even forget the difficulties they had had in coping with different approaches to learning.

Whereas there was no point in denying the value of their retrospective accounts a complementary strategy of investigating the initial expectations of newly arrived overseas students presented itself. This second survey provided some opportunity for checking what overseas students expected to experience. The relevant details on teaching and learning are reported here.

Altogether 112 overseas students completed a simple, focused questionnaire. As the respondents were drawn from a number of educational programmes, embracing an open invitation 'Welcome Weekend' for a large number of overseas students, two pre-sessional language and orientation courses, a B.Ed. bridging course for experienced schoolteachers (mostly from Hong Kong), and two masters' level courses, it is pointless detailing the sample profiles. It is sufficient to state that, although it is impossible to claim a strict representative-ness, those completing the questionnaire were drawn from a worldwide geogra-phy of recruitment, were studying at both undergraduate and postgraduate levels, some of considerable work and professional experience, and were roughly of equal numbers of men and women.

We regarded the data as a general picture of what some overseas students were thinking as they prepared themselves for different courses of study in two British universities.

Starting with their academic hopes and fears, not surprisingly the acquisition of knowledge, academic development and success were high on their personal agendas, counterbalanced by the fears associated with failure and 'losing face' and experiencing communication problems in a foreign language and different academic system. It was clear that overseas students were very motivated to succeed and make the most of the opportunities, while being alive to the likely difficulties.

Given the limitations of the sample representativeness, it is still useful to detail the full range of responses to these academic hopes and fears questions, which are shown in Table 2.2 ranked in numerical priority order. There is nothing remarkable about these findings as it would be reasonable to expect hopes to outweigh fears at the outset of a course of study and for ideas of success to be wrapped around academic achievement concerns. Moreover the overseas students' expectations were firmly fastened to the vocational relevance of their studies for work roles back in their own country.

As the thrust of the research project was focused around learning experiences it was considered necessary to examine in more detail particular aspects of the learning process, notably essay and assignment writing, discussion-based learning and the overseas students' perceptions of their personal adjustments to learning in a different academic and cultural milieu. Once again in reporting the findings it is only necessary to highlight the main points.

With regard to essay and assignment writing, on the whole students seemed positive about the task, which for many forms the centre of their academic studies. Some were anxious to have clear guidelines and much help with what they saw as a new activity or which varied from their previous educational experience. On the other hand others saw essay writing and the like in the British university system as an opportunity to be free from the spoon-feeding they had previously experienced and as a chance to pursue their own interests. Where students anticipated writing difficulties it was mainly in the context of dealing with the complexities of a foreign language or in an academic style that was unfamiliar to them.

The variety of courses represented in the expectations survey differed in the extent to which a discussion-based approach to learning was prominent – more in the arts and humanities and less in the science and technology subjects. For those subjects where discussion was central it was seen as a definite aid to understanding, particularly of difficult aspects of a subject requiring extensive explanation and where the free exchange of ideas stimulated fresh thinking. Discussion in the latter sense was seen to broaden personal perspectives as well as the capacity to communicate more effectively and develop the powers of

Table 2.2   Academic hopes and academic fears among newly arrived overseas students at both universities

Academic hopes		Academic fears	
• Acquisition of knowledge, academic development and successful completion	67 responses	• Fear of failure	24 responses
• Obtain academic qualifications	44	• Inadequacy of English language ability	8
• Develop English language skills	43	• Coping with teaching and learning and coursework demands generally, such as:	5
• Make the most of opportunities	10	• passing examinations;	4
• Develop skills in different approaches to teaching and learning	10	• communication with lecturers;	3
• Update specialized professional knowledge and expertise	10	• inadequate basic knowledge;	8
• Prepare for more advanced study	9	• new learning styles;	2
• Enjoy the intellectual atmosphere	9	• self-discipline;	2
• Acquire relevant knowledge and skills to aid development in home country	6	• too much pressure of work;	2
• Enhance promotion prospects	3	• choosing options;	2
• Develop good relationships with academic tutors	1	• not enough practical experience;	1
		• difficulty of returning to study;	1
		• personal adjustment problems interfering with study	1

self-expression. Considering that this meant competency in a foreign language the value of discussion as a very personal learning experience should not be underestimated.

On the organization of discussion, several students were anxious about the size of groups and the opportunity to effectively participate in a form of learning that was highly regarded in universities. Related comments to the effect that the induction of students into the discussion process had to be sensitively handled and gently eased showed an awareness of its value as an aid to learning and a positive anticipation of its benefits. This is noteworthy because very few overseas students claimed previous experience of the discussion-based approach, even amongst those from European countries.

It should also be noted that Arab students seemed uninterested in the discussion approach whereas a sophisticated view came from a Hong Kong teacher to the effect that discussion 'is just one avenue in the learning experience. Experiential approaches are also important, perhaps even more so for those whose native language is something other than English.'

The personal adjustments overseas students felt they might have to make have already been noted in passing. Most students responding to this question anticipated having to make adjustments, with the usual mix of positive feeling and some anxiety. In addition to the expected adjustments to new teaching and learning methods the knowledge that they would have to become more self-reliant was on their minds.

For some the enormity of the leap is exemplified in the following statement, again from a Hong Kong teacher undertaking the B.Ed. course:

> In Hong Kong we were taught by the teacher. During primary and secondary education teachers taught us what he wanted us to learn. The work I needed to do for studying was to remember all the things which was told by the teacher and finish all the exercises that they told me to do . . . Now it is quite different . . . The lecturer will not teach all the subject knowledge . . . I need to find many references from the library and study them myself. I will discuss with other schoolmates . . . We will learn from each other . . . The most important point from studying at universities is that I must learn by myself . . . No more teach by the teachers [sic].

Overall there was no indication that students feared making changes. One Japanese student expressed a very relevant perspective:

> The English education is very useful for research. In other words students spend a lot of time in expressing their ideas . . . but Japanese students spend most of their time in absorbing the knowledge and don't spend their time on how to use the knowledge. In the case of research work, the English method of training is more effective than that of Japan.

In summarizing both the reflections of overseas students looking back on their studies and the expectations of those looking forward, the quality of the contact with the academic tutor was crucial in making the learning experiences positive and developmental. The emphasis on relationships was seen as a key means of coping with adjustment and change, whether of an academic kind or in the personal domain. Their need for help from academic tutors as exemplars of the system of higher education and learning was seen as both an instrumental one, for the acquisition of knowledge and qualifications, and expressive, in terms of enabling them to express their thoughts effectively.

To complete these perspectives from the standpoint of the overseas students' learning experiences, actual and anticipated, it is necessary to outline the results of the intensive interviews with postgraduate research students, a special group outside the surveys.

Altogether 23 research students were interviewed from both universities, representing most faculties but predominantly in the sciences. Only four women students were interviewed. The geographical spread was evenly distributed across the continents.

The common thread of experience amongst research students of differing background experience and stages of completion was the necessity of a self-sustaining motivation, quite like those students of UK origin. It seems as if overseas research students do experience special difficulties though. Amongst these is the barrier of language which has to be overcome with a high degree of self-directed and rather isolated private study. Of particular difficulty was the preparation of research reports written at a suitable level of technical English using refined, conceptual language. Becoming more familiar with the English language through everyday experience was only partially helpful in these technical matters.

But the most significant factor in the learning experiences of overseas research students was the nature of the relationship with their academic supervisor. This has already been noted with regard to students undertaking taught courses. The importance of this relationship will be analysed in more depth from the perspective of cross-cultural expectations, but it is helpful at this point to stress its significance within the broader picture of the British university system. For many overseas students, teaching and learning were centred on *individual* academics – the gatekeepers of this system.

In the minds, but not often in the experiences of overseas research students, is the image of the ideal supervisor. This person was seen as taking the initiative, and after more than meeting the often disoriented student halfway, setting out to establish a strong bond along the lines of 'guide, philosopher and friend', referred to earlier.

What was desired was considerable guidance at the initial stages of a research project, not only specifically related to the academic task but also in gaining access to learning facilities such as computers, libraries, laboratories, and, above all, the resource staff. In the supervision process the ideal was represented as someone who provided considerable structured guidance, especially at the early stages of a research project, complete with comprehensive feed-back through regular tutorial discussions. This graduated induction was seen as the most desirable means of easing the research student into proper self-responsibility for their own learning upon a more certain foundation of confidence.

In the interviewed sample of research students some were very happy with their supervision, which was primarily attributed to the establishment of good personal rapport. This was made up of personal interaction underpinned by the feeling that the supervisor had a positive attitude towards providing support. The most successful supervisors were those who could empathize with the needs of the students and make good academic judgements of how best they should be supported without creating dependency.

Students who had a less happy relationship with their supervisors felt that they had real difficulty in comprehending that overseas students might know very little about how to do research. The tendency by supervisors to take things for granted in an unfamiliar academic culture for many overseas students was seen to cloud the relationship from the outset. The enabling or gatekeeping function of supervisors, allowing students fully to benefit from their time at university, broke down if the relationship was clouded in this way.

All the interviewees felt that a knowledge of their home country was an important asset for supervisors, and in many instance this was missing. This problem was compounded by the frequent reference to British perspectives and inside knowledge which was outside the experience of overseas students.

Gaining regular access to supervisors was a common problem. For many, diffidence in seeking regular supervision and asking for simple things was also a problem. To some extent these difficulties were mitigated by self-help groups and informal support from British research students. But these were regarded as secondary strategies and a compensation for what they really wanted.

To complete the overseas students' perspectives on their learning experiences two summary points stand out. The first is the need and the expectation that they will receive a good deal of high quality personal attention from academic tutors and supervisors. Most overseas students come to British universities feeling uncertain about their own knowledge and ability, and even as a person. The quality of their interaction with academics, as key gatekeepers in the higher education system, is crucial to their sense of security and motivation to succeed as well as the specifics of their need to know and learn effectively. All the overseas students were embarking upon a special form of status passage experience, charged with a high level of personal risk and vulnerability, and every step along the route to successful completion is difficult and challenging. Just like the thousands of mature adults returning to learning, taking up second-chance opportunities, overseas students represent a special category of need whom the universities have a moral duty to help. The fact that they are also paying a high economic price puts them in the bracket of customers with a right to expect good service.

The second point, which is dealt with more fully in other chapters, is that the social and cultural context of their experience as overseas students is also of considerable importance. Study is often a lonely pursuit and the need for supportive others around, as well as a good experience of living in a foreign culture, goes a long way to offset the pains of adjustment and change.

Attention turns now to the perceptions and experiences of university academics, in their dealings with the teaching and learning exchange with overseas students.

Any relationship between teachers and learners is bound to be complex. The needs and expectations of overseas students generate special difficulties and demands for university teachers. This point will be developed shortly. But it is also worthwhile noting that perhaps overseas students are not that more difficult to teach than mature students returning to full-time study after several years working or conventional-age students with no real experience of life to call upon. The point of difference is relative and difficult to define percisely. Because overseas students are arriving in greater numbers than hitherto and from countries with little previous connection with British education it is inevitable that they should be viewed as separate and different and presenting special problems for those who teach them. Yet the point could be stretched too far.

None the less, our special focus was on overseas students as learners, viewed from the standpoints and experiences of university teachers, a general term embracing the different roles of lecturer, demonstrator, supervisor, tutor and other ways of facilitating learning. The research approach meant that our sample was drawn from those with plenty of experience of teaching overseas students, by no means every university academic, and within those departments with an energetic overseas student recruitment policy. These wide-ranging and intensive interviews were often anecdotal and impressionistic, yet based on real experience and clearly touching upon deeply held values and ideas in the minds of academics. While this section of the chapter is not as detailed as the preceding part the essentials of the data certainly identify some key issues that have transpired from the recruitment of overseas students to university courses across a broad range of subjects and levels of study.

The data is approached in two stages. First, specific aspects of teaching and learning, as perceived by university staff, are illustrated as a grounding for the second stage, attention to general issues about the role of academics in the current policy context of increased overseas recruitment.

As the overseas students' experiences showed there was an expressed need for academics to be cast in a personal and very supportive role. Obviously not every overseas student has such an expectation but with high fees being paid there is evidence of a growing demand for consumer satisfaction. One vital form of satisfaction is in the expectation that the need for such a high quality interpersonal relationship, as part of a total educational package, is an obligation to be met by academics and the university in general.

This expectation, which we have presented as a reasonable one for overseas students to hold, conflicts with the real-world concerns of academics. As one of the respondents claimed, 'Perhaps responsible recruiters should put more emphasis on the fact that British universities are not primarily teaching establishments.'

Most academics are concerned with their research and publications track-record, which lies at the heart of career promotion and status. Of course, there is professional integrity and pride to be had from effective teaching and super-vision, but it has lower priority amongst academics. This general issue lies behind the day-to-day issues of teaching and learning, to which attention now turns.

At that level of operation some academic respondents felt unduly pressed by the needs of overseas students for a great deal of time and attention. The issue is summarized in the following remark by a senior lecturer: 'Their [overseas students] money is accepted but departments make no provisions for the additional demands on resources – such as staff time – which their special academic needs create.'

Overall, commitment was uneven, ranging from a positive response to overseas students' needs far beyond the call of duty, to a 'received-on-sufferance approach'. The greatest demand came at the beginning of the academic year, when most staff are fully stretched with an influx of students and plenty of administration, as well as the initiating processes of introductory teaching and supervision. Bewildered overseas students, some of whom arrive just after the beginning of the academic year because of bureaucratic delays, constitute a real problem for those hoping for a smooth start. Such irritations magnify the view of overseas students as needy and demanding.

The regular causes of the time and attention needs are what might be expected such as help with the English language; lack of familiarity with the subject and, by implication, the culturally specific nature of the background context; different experiences of learning and teaching; fears of losing face and being inhibited from active participation; over-reliance on tutors and so forth.

It should be noted, however, that some academics had developed teaching strategies for dealing with the needs of overseas students on a positive problem-solving basis. Despite the perception that overseas students created extra work burdens, these academics had approached their students at the outset and were sensitive to the tutor's role as interpreter of the system for the student.

A specific example was based on the recognition that rote learning, didactic teaching in a 'spoon-fed' system and a lack of hands-on experience were at the root of many overseas students' study and learning difficulties but that a concerted approach by a department to anticipate these was possible:

> Putting students right on the British academic approach needs early activation. We have a departmental policy. Early course-work is planned so that there is no unique solution. Small, mixed nationality groups toss the topic around and have to hand in the results very early for assessment. This sets the scene for independent thinking and self-responsibility though they continue to need plenty of feedback. If departments do not uncover deficiencies and develop lateral thinking early on they are failing their students.

But the fact that such comments were exceptional underlines the general point that overseas students as rather a burden in the teaching and learning domain was the more common view.

The learning problems of overseas students was strongly felt in research-based programmes, where it was frequently remarked that it cannot be assumed that students with even a good honours degree from an overseas university have been adequately prepared to cope with the demands of postgraduate study. As a result, supervisors can find they have to spend considerable time filling in gaps in students' knowledge.

This issue seemed to stem from the larger one concerning academic selection policy and practice. The policy of selection and admissions of overseas students as operated by individual academics varied considerably, according to their own ideas of what constituted fairness and inside knowledge of different educational systems.

One admissions tutor, for example, claimed that his awareness of different national systems of education enabled him to make judgements about the relative attainments of the Chinese in Malaysia and Singapore and between other ethnic groups in these countries. These rule-of-thumb judgements are hard to challenge. A more prickly issue arises over the impositions of admission quotas for home students and an open market for overseas student recruitment to generate income. This practice provoked several comments about the effect on courses, particularly research-based ones.

In some research-based programmes, where funding has fallen to low levels, the demand by high-calibre home students competing for few places is intense. At the same time some departments are accepting overseas students of questionable academic background and potential in order to just maintain a research profile. As a result there can be a gap between two ability groups, with the most able being home students and the least able overseas students.

There is considerable pressure on staff to help the least able catch up the most able, which is obviously very time-consuming. As one academic pithily remarked: 'We used to have a department full of good students. Now we have one or two really high fliers and then the rest, all oddballs of one kind or another.'

The question of standards was seen to be magnified wherever a high proportion of overseas students were recruited to a course or department. For some academics, though, this was a small price if universities could be lifted out of their complacency and ethnocentrism and reflect in a real way the internationalism of universities. But the reluctance by other academics to see overseas students as an opportunity to improve teaching and learning approaches was evident in some courses by the ways in which a mixed ethnic group was handled. In certain courses where mixed groups had to be subdivided the groupings were on home/overseas lines and fostered some resentment by the latter. Sometimes this happened by design but also by accident through alphabetical listing where it was often the case that overseas students' surnames cluster together more.

It would appear that the failure to regard overseas students as individuals, treating them instead as indistinguishable members of a common group, aggravates the issues of selection and standards, without addressing the challenge to change teaching and learning approaches. At the same time it is clear that the thrust towards income generation by overseas student recruitment had resulted in lower standards in research-based courses, as perceived by some academics.

The central point that emerges from this glimpse into academic views and experiences was the norm of the 'goodwill factor'. This attitude appears to hold the middle ground between those whose teaching and learning strategies have been challenged and improved by the needs of overseas students and those whose purpose is to take avoiding action and minimize contact. It is possible to dignify the latter position on the traditional grounds that teaching and learning revolve around the largely self-reliant process of reading for a degree instead of being taught. The needs of overseas students for a great deal of teaching and learning support is seen to dominate the traditional pursuit of academic excellence, which relies far less on a teaching culture and much more on a community of independent scholars learning by themselves.

For those taking on the demands of needy overseas students, out of a sense of duty, for professional reasons, or as 'goodwill', the underlying issue is the extent to which these factors are recognized by senior management.

The feeling that emerged from the interviews, with other staff as well as academics, is that goodwill is taken for granted. Goodwill may prove to be fragile in the face of continual cutbacks, increased demands from higher levels of overseas student recruitment and, most tellingly, from an awareness that those who fail to respond to the additional needs of overseas students continue to flourish in the system.

The goodwill factor points up inherent contradictions of policy and practice which is expressed most clearly in the role of the academic. Basically the hard truth is that there seems to be little bonus in teaching overseas students or taking a real interest in their personal lives. Certainly there was no career advantage in being an effective teacher or supervisor of those whose needs were greatest. Expressed simply by one academic: 'Departments are rewarded for recruiting overseas students. Individuals in departments are not rewarded for teaching them.'

Taking this idea further, it was frequently remarked that teaching and particularly tutoring are not highly regarded or rewarded by the university system, therefore many academics are reluctant to spend too much time on such activities at the expense of research, involvement in working parties, inter-university, and other extra-university activities which carry a higher prestige value and therefore contribute to promotion prospects in a way that teaching and tutoring do not. So when the extra demands of overseas students are imposed on staff at the same time as extra demands by the UGC grant criteria for more research and outside liaison together with a worsening staff–student ratio, declining morale and a poor outlook for university financing in the future, then cynicism and resentment are perhaps almost inevitable. For such reasons it should not be surprising to find that academic staff who still value and live to the idea of career mobility avoid becoming too involved with the time-consuming demands of the overseas student.

This rigidity and contradiction in the nature of the academic role, highlighted by the needs of overseas students and the climate of adversity that has characterized British universities in recent years, requires a radical overhaul. As a matter of fairness, good teaching must be seen to be rewarded with the tangible accolade of promotion or at least equal opportunity for career advancement. This might even encourage academics to take on more teaching and regard it more seriously as a hallmark of professionalism. At present there is an unbridgeable gap between teaching and research, whereas they should be indivisible in higher education. This fault is caused by the university system with its obsessive striving to create status differences and hierarchies and refusal to evenhandedly value the communication of knowledge through teaching.

At the same time the universities, in their struggles to generate income and survive, have partly succeeded through enterprising ventures, of which a notable one is overseas student recruitment. Yet, as this study shows, the problem lies in the capacity of the infrastructure of services to cope with their special needs. Whilst the policy of recruiting more overseas students has its rationale in increased revenue, individuals in continual contact with these students have indicated that high quality provision can only be achieved through an appropriate back-up in the form of staffing and money to underpin any initiatives and provide good quality support. Clearly there is a great deal of learning going on by university staff at all levels and this is matched by goodwill and concern for the needs of others. But these elements, important as they are, are no substitute for more resources to improve the delivery of services in support of the relationship between academic and overseas student. Probably overseas students will still make demands on academics for personal support, as well as learning support, but this task is made easier by a sound infrastructure.

Even if this issue were corrected, it would not by itself deal with the nature of the exchange in the teaching and learning domain. Two factors are of central importance. The first, and perhaps the more difficult, is an attitude of mind. This is evidenced in this study by the existence of the goodwill factor where those with positive attitudes regarded overseas students as both a challenge to professional abilities and personal responsiveness as well as living witness to the international outlook of university traditions and values. The vexed question is whether such attitudes can be instilled in others, or, better still, adopted by volition. There seems little point in attempting to train academics into a frame of mind, which is essentially a matter of personal choice balanced against perceived career advantage and strategy.

None the less, there seems to be some scope for training and professional development in an area of activity that calls for fresh knowledge and skills in teaching and learning and other aspects of interpersonal relations. Second, behind these immediate concerns of training and development lies the much larger issue of communication between members of the university: from senior to junior; academic to administrator and service personnel; department to department and so on. The study has noted the very *ad hoc* way in which experiences in dealing with overseas students are patchily learned, principally because there is no system for communicating such knowledge, within the university. The result of this can be the repetition of well-known mistakes and a failure to learn quickly enough – in short, an amateur approach to the needs of overseas students rather than a professional, well-informed one. Implicit in this adherence to amateurism is the neglect of the role of training for new roles and learning situations. As one academic remarked, 'It is the university which must change. We must put our own house in order.'

There is a need for training and support at all levels. Staff should be helped to understand the experiences which overseas students need if they are to benefit fully from their stay. Staff should also be enabled to move forward into areas not originally demanded of them, for example, in organizing and managing resources and analysing English language needs. To this list should be added the skills of supervision, counselling, and roles with new complexities such as admissions tutor, course promotor and marketer, in addition to understanding the roles and functions of others in support capacities.

Staff and home students must receive encouragement to gain in sensitivity so that ethnocentrism has no place in an international community of learners. Unfortunately the low priority given to training for *all* staff, not just those being inducted as recent employees, is one which is likely to discourage learning, flexibility and development amongst staff and in this sense contribute to a lack of dynamism and collaboration in the university as a whole.

This chapter has demonstrated a sympathy towards the needs of overseas students, as consumers with rightful expectations of high quality support, particularly in the teaching and learning arena. The assumption has been that it is the professional duty of academics to pay proper attention to teaching and learning, for all kinds of students, not just those from overseas. Indeed, overseas students illustrate a major problem in university life for it is quite clear that teaching and learning do not have as much priority in the academic mind as research and publication, the traditional hallmarks of success in a career profile, in spite of the mobility blockages experienced in the past decade or so.

In that regard we have a natural sympathy, as university academics, with the inherent conflict and tension between the open-ended demands of teaching and learning, that is, helping others to learn effectively, and the pursuit of the kudos and status that derives from research and publication, or even the power to be exercised on the administrative and organizational front. If there is a 'fault' in the system the problem lies in the innate conservatism of universities to change their ways. Necessity has forced universities to generate income through, amongst other things, overseas student recruitment, not a deep-seated internationalism or a service mentality. This 'fault line', as it were, shows up clearly in the infrastructure problems associated with the market approach to educational provision in a system that is slow to learn in a deep and lasting way. At the heart of any change must be a wilful climate within such complex organizations that shifts the values and practices of academics towards a more co-operative relationship, both within the profession and generally amongst the whole community of scholars. Anything less is just rhetoric.

Reference

1. G. A. Brown and M. Atkins, *Effective Teaching in Higher Education*, London, Methuen, 1988, p. 1.

3

The Student–Tutor Relationship

Joanna Channell

Introduction

The focus of this chapter is the relationship of overseas students to their personal tutors. Taking into account the varying practices of different departments in the two institutions, this means the member of staff to whom the student is allocated, or to whom they have been told to turn for individual help. It emerged strongly from our research that most students see this as a key relationship. It became clear when we compared our student and our tutor data that the two groups bring to the relationship two very different sets of expectations of each other. These expectations, on either side, are conditioned by the previous cultural experiences of the two groups. Hence we were able to identify mismatches in expectation, leading to misinterpretation of the other's behaviour, as a cause of difficulty in the student–tutor relationship. Data on these mismatches constitute the principal content of the chapter, which focuses on one aspect of the more general issues on teaching and learning with overseas students reviewed in Chapter 2. More general information about overseas students' learning is available.[1]

What has emerged from the data is that we may characterize the relationship under four distinct, but highly related headings. These are:

1. The conventions of British higher education and their expression in the nature of the course or research which the student is undertaking, that is to say, broadly, those aspects of the relationship which are strongly influenced by constraints external to the two individuals, factors imposed by the institution as a system. Contrasted with that are three headings which are more individual and more under the control of particular students or tutors. They are nevertheless highly influenced by this first characteristic.
2. Tutor availability.
3. Personal rapport.
4. The academic relationship.

Before looking at each of these in detail, let us first characterize a rather general aspect of the perceived relationship, which is that overseas students at our two universities appeared to revere and have high expectations of tutors, and that tutors with experience of teaching overseas students were quite aware of this. (Note that comments taken from interviews, such as those of the two lecturers below, are reported in the form recorded by our interviewers, and are not necessarily direct quotes because we did not tape-record our interviews.)

> While doing research on assignment I'll have new experience to consult and to get on with well-qualified tutors and lecturers. (Newly arrived B.Ed. student, who completed a questionnaire on expectations of university)

> . . . I am also interest [sic] in knowing how the lecturers and tutors study deeply in their own areas. The ways, the approaches and the spirits they own and behave may stimulate me . . . I think not only their methodology and their academic achievements are significant to me but more valuable may be their attitude of learning and their ways of thinking are striking to me. (B.Ed. expectations)

> Home students are expecting and are expected to question and make their own decisions. Many overseas students come from regimes where they are expected to revere the lecturer and do what he tells them. (Lecturer, Science)

> . . . tend to place staff on a pedestal. (Lecturer, Engineering)

Hence, overseas students are likely to see their tutor as the best person to turn to for help with *everything*. In our leavers' questionnaire, we asked whether subjects had sought help with a learning problem, and if they had, who had they asked. Results were as in Table 3.1. This does not show that students consulted tutors more than they consulted all other forms of help, but it does show that tutors were preferred to friends, and to other forms of help such as hall wardens and student counsellors. We found, correspondingly perhaps, that the general message from our staff interviewees was 'overseas students are harder work' (that is, harder work than home students):

> There is no doubt that there is a greater time commitment to overseas students. Some lecturers would prefer not to have the additional problem of overseas students and prefer home students. (Adviser, Engineering)

> Often on arrival students expect very detailed help – expect supervisor to meet them and drive them around to find accommodation – but this is not the expectation of supervisors, 'and I would tell them to push off if they asked me'. (Lecturer, Science)

Table 3.1   Seeking help with learning problems

	Yes	Who? Tutor	Who? Friend	Who? Other
Loughborough ($n = 61$)	25	17	13	10
Nottingham ($n = 97$)	56	47	41	19

He felt that overseas students were very ready to seek help and could lead to staff feeling pressurized. (Lecturer, Engineering)

Overseas students' expectations of supervisors are different – expect supervisor to be their total helper and adviser. (Lecturer, Science)

Just with these opening general observations, we have come across expectations and impressions which are likely to pose problems in the working relationship of students and their tutors. While 'placing lecturers on a pedestal', may be no bad thing in the learning relationship, it is certainly not the prevailing attitude among British students, and hence not an attitude that British lecturers are likely to feel comfortable with. We notice also that, importantly, it seemed to go hand in hand with a sense of dependence on tutors which is not manifested by home students (even if they feel it). Expecting a lot of help and support seems to lead directly to the staff impression that students from overseas are harder work, over-demanding and so on. Hence we may expect a defensive attitude on the part of tutors who work with overseas students, and this is borne out by some (but by no means all) of the comments that follow.

1   The conventions of British higher education

In this section I illustrate and discuss expectations and attitudes that arise from the education system and ways in which courses and research are organized within it. Essentially what I mean here are expectations that arise from the system and modes of education being practised in the institution. That is to say, constraints that are to a certain extent exterior to the one-to-one relationship of the student and the tutor. Examples of relevant external constraints would be:

course aim
course syllabus
assessment method(s)
resource requirements (equipment, laboratories, books)
teaching styles
entry qualifications required
number of tutees per tutor
tutor's work load
institution's policy on, and attitude to, overseas students
department's policy on, and attitude to, overseas students (not necessarily the same as institution's)
number of home versus overseas students in department/course

In considering the effects of 'the system' on the student–tutor relationship we need, obviously, to distinguish between undergraduate work, taught postgraduate work, and postgraduate research, because of the different conventions associated with these different types of study.

Taught courses

Considering both types of taught courses, our general finding is that our overseas students find courses, assignments and reading very much less structured than they would like:

> Friends who have been doing [x (MA)] course had great trouble because the course consisted of a few lectures but mostly the students have to work on their own with no guidance for reading or work. (Leaver, interview)

> With perhaps only one lecture a week plus a vague reading list, they felt their study had no direction. (Group interview, students from USA)

> Thinks there is too much vagueness about the [M.Sc.] project and is uncertain about what he should be doing. (Leaver, interview)

> More personal tutorials. More supervision of coursework. (Suggestions at the end of the questionnaire)

> Sometimes I find it very difficult to know what we are expected to do in our assignments. More elaboration and guidance should be given. It's a waste of time guessing and trying to find out what we should write about. Moreover I hope we should be provided with more reference for our work. We should not be left roaming about in the library looking for our own books . . . We students from Hong Kong are not acquainted with learning by ourselves. (Education student, questionnaire on expectations)

> I know in university, study is to develop a person for thinking and creativity both in mind and concept. But lack of writing experience, I am afraid that I cannot express myself properly . . . so more guidance instructions are needed. (Education student, questionnaire on expectations)

The foregoing comments relate to perceptions of the nature of the learning task, and the learning styles students had previously encountered in other countries whether at school or at university. This student showed that he recognized a cultural difference:

> Thinks maybe he expects to be spoon-fed more than the lecturers are prepared to do; on the other hand maybe some of the lecturers don't make much effort to make themselves clear and help students to understand. (Leaver, interview)

And some staff drew attention to this in a similar way:

> They need hand-feeding. (Lecturer, Engineering)

> For students with a technical background, it is difficult to get them to think out a problem – they have a 'you tell me what you want and I'll do it' approach. (Admissions Tutor, Engineering)

Here it seems that misperceptions arise from one of the major characteristics of British higher education – its emphasis on self-reliance and self-directed study, with minimal control by staff. The basic idea is that life-skills training in finding information, understanding and presenting it will be fostered by issuing challenges and creating goals which students are free to meet in their own ways. Almost all teaching staff in British higher education have undergone the home system in their own education. Hence their expectation is that their own students will experience the same. These teachers find the reverence and lack of independence of some of their overseas students quite unacceptable. The students on the other hand may have previously experienced a variety of educational styles. Judging from their comments, their experiences are often of systems in which they are much more closely controlled and directed in what to do and when and how to do it. Hence in the British system they feel lost, lacking direction and generally insecure.

Research students

For research students there are similar difficulties with mismatched expectations, but they are perhaps sometimes exacerbated by the fact that research students, because they already have one degree, expect, and are expected, to be able to create their own study structures, but in fact many had found this very hard. Research students interviewed at Loughborough expressed the need for an induction programme on how to obtain information, how to use it, and what to do with it. Previous independence in the work situation was no guarantee of intellectual independence on returning to the student role. Research students who had been at Loughborough before were not necessarily in a happier position. They said that they carried an image of the department as it was when they left. Many changes had taken place which immediately made them feel disoriented. They had not worried about their coming at all since they thought of themselves as returning. The shock was therefore actually at least as great as for a newcomer when they discovered that, as research students, *nothing* was the same. They realized how much they had related to their course. Without a course to relate to, they felt totally alone. The nature of the supervisor–student relationship became absolutely crucial. All said that at first no other reference point was provided. Supervisors, because they knew these students had been in the department before, at once took everything for granted.

It has been said that in most British institutions assumptions seem to be made about all postgraduate students whether home or overseas. They have a degree already, therefore they must be able to cope. Several British former students, both recent and past, are on record as saying that they never felt such a part of their postgraduate surroundings as they did of their undergraduate surroundings (assuming a change of institution). At least they could take the cultural environment for granted. For overseas research students without the shared set of assumptions about the environment, uncertainties and the feeling of isolation are intensified. By contrast a Polymer Technology Department research student from Iraq had no such misgivings. It is interesting to consider that this department did not have any undergraduates, so all the students were 'new' at postgraduate level. The department was quite small and both course and research members of it commented on the ease with which the two worked side-by-side. As a laboratory-based subject there was 'always someone around'. Other interviewees at Loughborough indicated that they had only their supervisor to relate to. For a variety of reasons they did not feel able to ask this supervisor every little question so they found they had to rely on friends to learn about many aspects of their work. In early days when they had not made friendships, this was particularly difficult.

The first six months of the life of a research student were generally agreed by the students to be the most crucial. One group of six students interviewed as a group at Nottingham had been in their work for just six months at the time of interview, and the different responses of group members were enlightening, both generally, and in connection with their expectations of their supervisors. Those with previous research experience were settled in to their work, but complete newcomers were either just beginning to make a serious start on their work or were in a state of depression and anxiety in the fear that they would never come to grips with the subject in order to make a start on their own work. One problem they identified as crucial was the issue of preliminary reading and the attitude of their supervisors towards this. The approach which asked students to go away and generally read up on the subject was not appreciated by the students and especially by those whose English was poor. The students wanted directed reading and felt that there was no reason why their supervisors could not draw up a short list of essential reading and development at the beginning. Others at a later stage in their research largely agreed with this view although they felt that there were merits in broader reading at the beginning to which they might return later – but they generally felt that a more directed approach to the literature would avoid the experience of feeling that the first six months were wasted and the anxiety and sometimes desperation felt by a few at the end of this time.

It seems that these reactions of research students can be related again to the idea of the supervisor on a pedestal, as well as to the less directed conventions of our system. Students saw supervisors as already knowing everything there was to know about the student's particular research area, and therefore able, as the students perceived it, to furnish precise guidance. It must appear to such students that supervisors wilfully withhold instructions for directed reading. The reality is that most supervisors know only something of the area to be researched, and expect precisely to increase their own knowledge through the student's research.

It is also worth noting that most of the comments made by overseas research students have equally been uncovered to a greater or lesser extent in research on home research students. Much such work is usefully summarized in Brown and Atkins, Chapter 6.[2] What needs to be said then is perhaps that the effects of *similar* perceptions are exacerbated for overseas students because of the disorientation of studying in another environment ('culture shock') and the extent to which their expectations differ from those of home students.

Thinking now of both groups of students, that is, taught and research, it was clear from their comments that some staff perceived the mismatches of expectations and the ensuing difficulties these might cause. It also often appeared that they judged the students' expectations negatively, rather than seeing them purely as the result of cultural differences:

> Some expect knowledge to be poured into them and do not regard lectures or tutorials as stimulation to further thought and self-development. (Lecturer)

Students, whether undergraduate or postgraduate, on the other hand, had no way of anticipating the difficulties ahead, as was shown by the responses of incoming students in the expectations surveys. The recently arrived Loughborough research students' comments reported above are also revealing. Asked to comment on their 'hopes and fears for their stay at university' there were only 5 mentions, in 122 questionnaires returned, of fear of inadequate help or guidance, or tutors not recognizing overseas students' needs.

Related to the expectation of 'spoon-feeding' was the academics' perception that overseas students, as compared to their British counterparts, were unprepared for the analytical thought required in most course and research programmes:

> They lack the skills of analysis. Previous education has been descriptive and repetitive. The use of data and evidence and its analysis is a problem area. (Lecturer, Social Sciences)

> For example, they do not question the data they obtain, so if left to their own devices they will perhaps use a correct method but obtain a crazy result and try to incorporate it in their findings. (Lecturer, Engineering)

This perception was found also by Wright in her work with postgraduate course students and their tutors at the University of Reading.[3,4]

Another key area where experienced tutors had found a strong need to readjust their expectations concerned what our research assistant called 'a cultural awareness of technology'. Tutors in a variety of departments told us that overseas students tend to have learned in a theoretical and paper-oriented way about technical subjects, while in Britain they are expected to know what things do and how they work and to have a general three-dimensional practical feel for the subject.

> You can put them in a lab with lathes and six months later they'd still be there not knowing what to do. (Admissions Tutor, Science)

He elaborated that,

> Kids in England know how to do things like change bike wheels, understand gears etc. but the overseas students haven't got that kind of background.

The senior technician in one engineering department felt that the students he came across preferred book learning to doing. Many students seem neither to understand nor to appreciate the need to know how machines work, only what they do. In another engineering department, one lecturer pointed out that this has a knock-on effect on the relationship with technicians. Home students will request exactly the equipment they require to set up their experiments, while overseas students will request 'the equipment' and expect the technicians to provide it. At least some of this perceived difference derived from the lack of resources in education in some Third World countries from which our students came. One science lecturer told us that he had recently been in Bangladesh and the equipment in the department was regarded as so precious that the professor kept it locked up in his office – this would be equipment in common use by undergraduates here, he said.

Several tutors we talked to were aware of the necessity to accommodate the different backgrounds of their overseas students. Generally they felt that *they* were doing this but that some of their colleagues showed shortcomings! For example:

Dr X thought that often British academics lacked awareness of these differences. Consequently, they could not appreciate what the overseas student was getting worried *about*. (Senior Lecturer, Engineering)

Golden rule for his staff – start instruction from the basics, never assume competence in manual skills. (Director of Centre, Engineering)

Teaching staff need training in how to move students from a state of dependency, how to get students talking and discussing, how to encourage Muslim women students to participate in male-dominated groups, how to get students to exercise self-responsibility. These things should not be left to chance. (Tutor)

So far, we have looked at aspects of the student–tutor relationship that derive from our culture and institutional practice in universities as places of learning and from the nature of academic work in Britain, that is, things at least to a certain extent imposed from the outside on the student and the tutor. Now I turn to aspects of the relationship that have more to do with the way that students and tutors as individuals act out their relationships to each other, that is, aspects that are less constrained by the system (though they still are) and are hence open to negotiation and personal preference. The first is availability – time given and how it is negotiated.

2 Tutor availability

In relation to time available with tutors, many were happy with their experience, some knew of other students who were not, and yet others had been dissatisfied:

He was taught in his maths group with six students – 3 overseas and 3 home but in Curriculum Development there was often a very large group, perhaps 40. In the group of 6 it was very nice. Plenty of contact with tutors and plenty of time to get to know each other. (Leavers, interview)

Had the course been up to expectations? 'Beyond my expectations . . . though it has been hard work.' She spoke very favourably about the Linguistics Department – appreciated the friendliness of the staff, their helpfulness and preparedness to help in every way and time given to students. Makes the point that it is a small department and easy to know everyone and be known by all the staff. (Leavers, interview)

In theory there are many tutors in University can give guidance [sic]. But due to the time factor, they can't give you much guidance in practice. I suggest that specified period should be allocated for personal tutorials rather than by appointment (Suggestions in the questionnaire)

'You know who are the senior lecturers and who are the junior ones.' Interviewer: 'Why?' 'They are all busy but the senior lecturers are always too busy to see you' (Leavers, interview)

The actual arrangements for academic tutorial help were the subject of many comments. It was pointed out that due to their former mode of education in a hierarchical structure, many overseas students would find it very difficult to approach a tutor despite blanket invitations to do so at the beginning of the course.

The research students who were interviewed also commented on the availability of supervisors. One student, for example, had just got started when his supervisor took a sabbatical, so he was working entirely alone. Had it not been for the ultimate intervention of his head of department, he would have wasted irretrievable time on a wrong track. On the other hand another student commented that he had been very anxious before coming to the university because he had heard that some students only see their supervisor once a month, but in fact this fear was unfounded as he saw his supervisor for a long session each week and could see him for some minutes each day if he wanted. In contrast to this, the absence of regular set supervisions produced much anxiety too. Many were not sure either when they ought or when they needed to approach their supervisor. Some interviewees had felt deferent and had not liked to approach their supervisor at all! The ideal supervisor was seen as one who, offered considerable structure and regular tutorials and discussions.

The perception of teaching staff, as I said earlier, is that students from overseas, at any level, require a greater input of time than British students. Tutors across a number of departments at Loughborough pointed to poor language ability, lack of study skills, limited practical expertise, slower learning curves, some absence of initiative, and above all an inability to cope with change, as being problems which engaged their time as supervisors. In consequence a large expenditure of time spent on supervision, quite often, some staff felt, unrecognized by either their peers or seniors, became a vexed issue.

Interviews revealed a disjuncture between senior policy-makers and the activators of policy on how the issue of ensuring supervision time should be tackled:

> In line with the Jarratt Report, Heads of Departments should become more managerial, choosing and motivating staff for full efficiency. Overseas students do take more time and effort but Heads must know what their academics are actually doing and must manage their time more efficiently. Things have got to move forwards. (Senior policy-maker)

> Their [overseas students'] money is accepted but departments make no provisions for the additional demands on resources – such as staff time – which their special academic needs create. (Senior lecturer)

In the event, commitment was uneven. Individual staff attitudes varied between a commitment far beyond that which duty dictated, and a 'received on sufferance' approach, but there was no doubt that academics were being asked to fulfil a role in co-operating with institutional requirements as well as fulfilling their specific departmental role. All interviewees agreed that demands on time were particularly heavy when overseas students first arrived, but again there were different interpretations of their obligations. The approach, 'I'm here to help, come and see me if you have any problems', was seen by some staff to offer support without encouraging dependence. However, others felt this side-stepped real commitment. Since many overseas students felt inhibitions which prevented them from seeing a tutor for fear of losing face, one tutor told us:

> It is vital to go to the student to offer practical help and pre-empt the formation of problems. Once they realize that I am available many come, really seeking reassurance. (Tutor)

Another said:

> My first few weeks are particularly hectic because I feel I must give time to my overseas students immediately. I can see why some tutors wait to be approached.

Some staff are obviously quite good at creating an impression of being very busy, and hence discouraging students from doing what the staff have in fact in the first instance encouraged them to do – 'come and see me whenever you have a problem'. One departmental administration officer, able to look objectively at the issue, commented:

> Individual tutors tend to make excuses about how busy everyone is, just at the beginning of the academic year. This is precisely when academic appraisal and consequent areas of help need sorting, particularly for one-year postgraduate students.

The students' comments show that some are aware of the dichotomy. Perception of availability on both sides is linked, of course, to attitudes and expectations about the general modes-of-learning points which were referred to above. If the expectation of the system is for students to learn independently and create their own structures, then they will not need much tutorial and supervision time. But students do not know, at least when they set out, that this is the learning style. And when they do find out, they still want to be told *how to do it*. So they still come back to wanting tutor support and hence tutor time.

One reason for availability problems can be traced to another characteristic of British higher education – the triple role which academics are contracted to perform: teaching, research and management. Each of these roles may be more or less emphasized in particular departments or by particular individuals, but in all cases teaching staff have an obligation to fulfil all three roles and to divide their time between them. Hence they feel antipathy towards any influence which disrupts the personal balance of the three roles that they operate. One such influence is perceived to be the demands of overseas students. Considering students, it needs to be understood that they may be quite unaware of the triple role academics fulfil. They see academic staff as their teachers, who should therefore be available to meet their needs.

Staff in one department at Loughborough, with a great deal of experience working with students from overseas, offered the following advice:

> Set boundaries on what you can and will do for them. Demands and expectations otherwise become limitless.

3 Personal rapport

This area is already being hinted at in some of the foregoing comments – what sort of personal rapport is there between a student and their tutor? Under this heading I have included points about attitudes to other cultures, ethnocentrism and racism. Again, there was a mixture of satisfied and dissatisfied customers. One satisfied student saw her good experience as a direct result of cultural difference:

> In Italy the lecturers are very stiff and it is not possible or expected for students to ask questions at lectures or in seminars for it puts lecturers off! Here she has noticed how much easier going the lecturers are and how they expect to be questioned and how easily they admit that they have problems which they invite the students to help solve. (Leavers, interview)

Two mature students highlighted the differences they had noticed between home and overseas students:

> The home students were negative in their attitudes towards the department and the lecturers – distrustful of them. She felt that as a mature student it was her role to know what she wanted out of the course and to make sure that she got it and saw no point in being so negative. She felt that

the lecturers in the School of [X] were exceptionally friendly and approachable so there was no problem there. (Leavers, interview)

For research students, with no other departmental reference point, the supervisor was, as has been mentioned, of vital importance. Some research students interviewed at Loughborough were very happy with their supervisors and made some useful comments as to why this should be so. They put above all the establishment of personal rapport. The most successful supervisors seemed to be those who really empathized with their students by ascertaining – without being judgemental – where their new research students actually were, academically. Students who had a less happy relationship with their supervisor thought that some found it difficult to comprehend that their new students really might not know *anything* about researching or about the tools and facilities needed to activate it. Other supervisors failed to appreciate that self-sufficiency and confidence were sapped by environmental differences. A tendency for supervisors to take things for granted in a British system which might be unfamiliar to overseas students, immediately clouded the relationship.

The ideal research supervisor was seen as one who, having established the personal relationship already discussed by moving towards the student, then offered considerable structure in the early stages, coupled with quite firm guidance and comprehensive feedback through regular supervisions and discussions. Interviewees, especially those new to Britain, felt that they needed to be eased into self-responsibility after its implications had been fully explained. They thought that emphatic supervisors would know when students were confident enough to initiate their own ideas and be self-responsible and capable of self-assessment. Dependence and consequent frequency of supervision might cease very quickly or not for some time. After that the supervisor would concentrate on developing and channelling the work of the student to maximum effect. The supervisor is thus seen as both a counsellor and a teacher: this dual role is very demanding and not easily achieved by all teaching staff. Our finding corresponds closely to the summary in Brown and Atkins (p. 122) that 'the most popular style was one which coupled personal warmth with professional guidance'.

Many postgraduate interviewees felt that a knowledge of their home country was an important asset for their supervisor. Undergraduates commented similarly:

Overseas students advisers should be overseas students or those who have enough knowledge of different cultures. (Leavers, questionnaire)

We need a specially appointed tutor. He must have Third World experience. (Leavers, questionnaire)

It was clear, however, that this felt need was recognized by some of the staff we interviewed:

He considered that generally British personnel who had not experienced different cultures at first hand were not able to advise since they could not appreciate the nature of the problems involved. (Senior Lecturer of overseas origin, Engineering)

It is not a formal requirement that staff should travel to sending countries but many have done so and this helps with understanding on both sides. (Lecturer, Engineering)

A strange environment, culture shock and the extra pressures to succeed which go with paying huge fees all cause loss of confidence. Tutors must read between the lines, but all this takes a lot of time. (Tutor)

On the other hand the awareness shown by some staff seemed to lead them into a certain cultural stereotyping. This is of course hard to avoid but it is certainly not useful and sometimes may be outrightly prejudicial to individual students' interests:

Indians and Pakistanis not generally engineering minded – Kenyans particularly good engineers – Nigerians seem to be hardest to deal with – most African students somewhat unreliable in terms of planning work, timekeeping – Filipinos, Chinese and Malays tend to have a more responsible attitude. (Senior Technician, Engineering)

This interviewee, however, showed his positive side in his list of suggestions for technical instructors:

Always check that they can actually do what they say they can do – put them in a wide variety of practical situations – win their confidence first of all by: showing you respect them, showing them that you won't laugh at them, particularly in front of their peers. Avoiding situations of potential loss of face is essential, praising them for good work.

A particular issue, broadly under the heading of personal relationships, concerned use of names. Different cultures have different conventions for style and use of names, and this causes misunderstandings, one example being:

In Ghana people remember other people's names and faces and once met in a social gathering one is considered an acquaintance and one is free to stop someone in the street and consider them as a friend. But in England people do not take the trouble to learn names and can never remember you – pass you in the street without apparently recognizing you and this sort of thing leaves you in confusion. Feature of a good teacher – one who knows and uses the names of their students. (Leavers, interview)

Both some staff and the 'system' seemed little able to come to terms with a different naming convention:

Gave example of the resistance of the University and the printing department to putting names of Chinese students with their surname first – this was not the way they have done things in the past – but the Chinese pointed out that the certificate might not be valid in Hong Kong if the family name was not right. He acted to put this right and had to go to the Registrar to solve it. (Senior academic)

A student who responded to the pilot questionnaire used at Nottingham described how during the whole of her three-year course, her personal tutor had never addressed her by any of her names. Her assumption was that he had never taken the trouble to learn to pronounce her slightly complicated first name.

Practically, the use of names to allocate alphabetically to tutor groups produced a possibly unfortunate effect:

He said that the Hong Kong students seem to be together a lot but then it emerged that when classes are divided up they are done alphabetically (i.e. the intake of c. 140 is treated as a whole) and so the Kongs and the Lams and the Wongs tend to find themselves together. (Lecturer, Medical School)

4   Academic relationship

From personal/cultural issues, I move to the last main heading, that of the nature of the academic relationship. Here, students' comments were on how they were taught, and importantly, on the nature and quantity of feedback they got from their tutors.

For research students more than for undergraduates the perception of their supervisor's academic knowledge and ability was important. Again here we may note a parallel with other findings on students generally. MacAleese and Welsh[5] found that research students chose the following four characteristics as most important in their supervisor: knowledgeable, available, helpful, stimulating. Some research students who reported themselves generally satisfied with the personal qualities of their supervisors and their availability for consultation, voiced doubts about the knowledge of supervisors and their capability for supervising particular projects. In such situations students had looked to other staff or research fellows to help them but there was a suggestion that supervisors were not good at referring them to alternative sources of help and advice and that it was something of a happy accident if a student found someone to help. One student gave an example of a problem he faced on his research which his supervisor was unable to help him solve. If it had not been for the appointment of a new member of staff, who had some knowledge of this area of work, he would never have solved the problem which had held up the progress of his work for six months. Another student commented that he had been given specific assurances that the department at the university had staff with expertise in his area. He found on arrival that this was not true – indeed his main complaint was that he found, on arrival in Britain, that the whole subject area in which he was interested was very undeveloped here. He felt very dissatisfied with all aspects of the work but particularly with the dishonesty about it.

Supervisors who were active in research were preferred to those 'who sit in their offices' since students had more confidence in their interest and their abilities. Interestingly, considering the many comments made about availability, it seemed that some research students were less concerned about the amount of time supervisors gave them than about the quality of help when they did get supervision. One student commented that his supervisor was the head of department and was also frequently out of the country, but when available he was really helpful.

One issue which we specifically asked about was academic feedback. We wanted information about both the quantity and the type of feedback received, and about whether it had been perceived as useful. The questionnaire to leavers asked about feedback, see Table 3.2. The respondents were asked to comment on feedback on academic work under three headings, as shown. From this we can see that while many of them were satisfied with the feedback they got, many also were not. There were also comments and suggestions about the nature of the feedback received. All types of comments revealed the general expectation of and felt need for a structured academic environment. It was to the academic tutor and to the department that students expected to relate and feedback on work standards was felt to be imperative. Several mentioned the depression they had suffered when work was returned with neither comments, suggestions, nor invitations to discuss it. Constructive feedback was seen as crucial before students could judge their performance and thus know how to proceed. Several students commented in interviews that difficulties they had experienced with academic work were not picked up quickly enough or at all. It was felt that if lecturers noticed a problem, they should take the initiative. In the event, students had to approach lecturers over any difficulties, by which time it might be too late.

The nature of feedback was commented on by students:

> For example when the student takes his ideas/draft etc. to a tutor he expects the tutor to be interested in it, criticize it, tear it apart if necessary, but generally the tutors don't seem to take it too seriously. They just put a few spelling and bits of grammar – but I could get a computer to do that so that's not what I want. I get the impression that my work is not valued – and it is the same for everyone. You are just expected to finish and that's it. There are no suggestions to improve and develop ideas – no real discussion aimed towards this kind of end. (Leavers, group interview)

Table 3.2   Feedback from tutors about written work (%)

Perception of feedback	Written comments		Suggestions for improvement		Discussion	
	Nottingham	Loughborough	Nottingham	Loughborough	Nottingham	Loughborough
Adequate	58	52	49	43	40	52
Inadequate	31	38	40	44	46	36
No response	11	10	10	13	13	12

She made the point that she wanted to see me to talk not on her own behalf, as she was very satisfied with experience here but on behalf of some others who were not. She pointed out that with essays, some of the lecturers gave them back and then found time to go through essays paragraph by paragraph making suggestions and giving help with development and she really appreciated this. Other staff just return the essays in the pigeon hole. (Leaver, interview)

Hence, students' suggestions in this area were concerned with setting up a more structured environment for specific feedback:

Strengthen the personal tutorial system (more compulsory or arranged meetings).

More personal tutorials, more supervision on coursework.

In my opinion individual guidance for coursework is very important.

A seminar tutor to be appointed (1 tutor to 5 students only) to advise students on coursework. We need help terribly.

The personal tutor as language teacher

For most overseas students, English is their second language. At our two universities, admissions regulations stipulated a requirement to show sufficient competence in English through particular recognized tests. (Further information on English language tests has been published[6] or is available from the British Council.) Furthermore both universities now provide pre-sessional English language courses as well as in-sessional support (though during our study the service was considerably less comprehensive than it now is). (Further information on such English teaching is available.[7-11] Even with the availability of these important services, we must recognize that there will be room for students' English to improve and that an important opportunity for hearing and speaking good English will be in individual contact with a tutor or supervisor. Students hope for this opportunity, and again here they have misplaced expectations. This time, however, their expectations arise not from cultural differences but from the simpler point of being non-native speakers of English. Their general belief is that because their tutor is a native speaker of English (and hence speaks English perfectly) it follows that s/he will automatically be able to act as a language teacher. Most academic staff are more than willing to help and to patiently correct students' English. But very few (outside of the specialist language/linguistics area) can explain, for example, exactly why examples like the following are incorrect!

I am in Britain since three months

or

I have coming to Britain to traning and study in Nottingham University in Department of X, and I would like to traning in the Department on some rigs and how to conceted with some instruments, how to measuring, calibration, Maintenance these equepment

Such work is the province of the specialist English language teacher. When tutors are unable to give detailed explanations, the students' reaction is that the tutor is unhelpful, while the tutor may confront uncomfortable feelings of inadequacy. Not a good recipe for successful rapport. The absence of specialist knowledge of English language may account for some of the students' negative comments on feedback, alluded to above. While it is quite sufficient on a home students' essay to draw a wiggly line and write 'style' or 'ugh' in the margin, non-native writers want more. They want to know *exactly* what they should have said and (worse) why. Giving guidance beyond the straightforward 'because it sounds right' or 'because that's the way we do it in lab reports/economics essays/M.Sc. dissertations in agronomy' is again the province of the discourse analyst.

In this connection, the advice I give to staff in training sessions on working with overseas students is the following:

1. Be clear that your greatest asset is your ability to give a model of good English. Have confidence in your judgement of what sounds right, and concentrate on giving feedback based on that.
2. Be clear to yourself and to your students that you are *not* a language teacher. *Never* give off-the-cuff explanations of the grammar or discourse rules of English – they are likely to be *wrong*!

Summary and conclusions

The research carried out on this subtopic of our programme, namely, the relationship of overseas students to their academic tutors, seems to show the following:

Overseas students, generally:

1. Both need, and desire, a higher level of tutor contact than they get in the British system;
2. Have difficulty with our unstructured system (i.e. multiple learning sources);
3. Feel misunderstood by tutors.

Tutors, on the other hand:

1. See overseas students as voraciously demanding of their time (even when they enjoy giving it and do so willingly);
2. See overseas students as overdependent – 'tell me what you want and I'll do it';
3. Are aware that their role is to encourage independence but don't always know how to do it, that is, by giving the right kind of feedback.

What action seems to be consequent upon this research? It leads, in one way, to proposing a rather general idea that everything would be perfect if we all knew much more about each others' cultures. But I believe it is hopelessly idealistic to propose that as a way forward. With relevance to our situation in British institutions of higher education, we cannot insist that all our staff travel abroad, or have the experience of studying abroad, or learn foreign languages. Some, as individuals, will travel abroad, and will broaden their cultural horizons, but some will not. Individuals in any society are the socio-cultural products of their own culture.

Helping students to get the most from relationships with tutors/supervisors can be achieved in two main ways: first by changing expectations, and secondly be clarifying actualities.

For students, their expectations need to be changed at the beginning of their study. They need to be tuned in to what they will *actually* find in the British system. This is achieved successfully through pre-study and orientation programmes which many universities and colleges now organize. In the absence of these and for students who are unable to attend them, the issues will have to be tackled soon after the commencement of their course of study and this is covered under the heading of 'Tutor availability'.

By 'clarifying actualities' I mean that tutors and supervisors need to make explicit to new students the nature of the working relationship they will have. Brown and Atkins refer to this as 'making a contract', and this is a useful way to think of it. Student and tutor both undertake to do certain things and hence each side is clear about the other's perceptions. This recalls clearly the staff comments on 'setting boundaries on what you will do for them'. It is also designed to release students from the anxiety of not knowing, which many in our study referred to. Informal headings for the content of this contract are such things as:

consultation arrangements – timings
                         lengths
                         how set up ('come and see me whenever you need
                         to' is too vague!)
content of consultations – (what can the tutor help with?)
tutor's expectations of the student

Brown and Atkins point out that a good working relationship cannot begin until a student is secure on such matters as accommodation, finance and travel. Our findings confirm that – but to a greater extent for overseas students. They suggest that positive steps towards personal rapport can be made by checking that such matters are in hand. This both clears the way for work to begin, and gives students the impression that their tutor has a caring attitude towards them.

So I see the consequent action as being taken in the area of staff training, which will be considered in detail in Chapter 5. The need is for interpersonal skills training for academic staff. Increasing these skills will enable them to continue to act as they are now in terms of time given to their students from overseas, but to be perceived in the way they do so as helpful, constructive and supportive.

References

1. G. M. Greenall and J. E. Price (eds), ELT Documents 109: *Study Modes and Academic Development of Overseas Students*, London, British Council, 1980.
   G. Williams, M. Woodhall and U. O'Brien, *Overseas Students and their Place of Study; Report of a Survey*, London, Overseas Students Trust, 1986.
2. G. A. Brown and M. Atkins, *Effective Teaching in Higher Education*, London, Methuen, 1988.
3. J. Wright, 'Intercultural postgraduate learning, the acquisition of study skills: an institutional response to the results of research, *International Journal for the Advancement of Counselling*, 8, 1985, 279–96.
4. J. Wright, 'The acquisition of research skills by postgraduates in UK universities', *Canadian Journal of Counselling*, 1986.
5. R. McAleese and J. Welsh, 'The supervision of postgraduate research students' in J. F. Eggleston and S. Delamont (eds), *Supervision of Students for Research Degrees*, Birmingham, BERA, 1983, pp. 13–22.
6. S. Davies and R. West, *The Pitman Guide to English Language Examinations*, London, Pitman Education, 1984.
7. A. P. Cowie and J. B. Heaton (eds), *English for Academic Purposes*, Reading, BAAL/SELMOUS, University of Reading, 1975.
8. Price J. (ed.), *Pre-Sessional English Language Courses in Britain Today*, Newcastle, University of Newcastle upon Tyne/SELMOUS/ETIC, 1978.
9. G. James, (ed.), *The ESP Classroom*, Exeter, Exeter Linguistic Studies, Vol. 17 1984.
10. J. McDonagh and A. French (eds), *The ESP Teacher: Role, Development and Prospects*, ELT Documents 112, London, British Council, 1981.
11. P. Robinson (ed.), *Academic Writing: Process and Product*, ELT Documents 129, London, Macmillan, 1988.

4

Living Needs

Helen Lewins

Concern for the living needs of overseas students was expressed as long ago as the latter half of the nineteenth century, when early welfare organizations were set up to help the increasing number of wealthy Indian students in Britain. These students were uninformed, unqualified and unprepared for life and study in Britain.[1]

Welfare services, largely run by voluntary organizations, continued to develop steadily,[2] but no dramatic developments occurred until the late 1940s and 1950s when the advent of a large number of overseas students without a European cultural background was seen to produce new 'problems', which were the subject of many subsequent studies.[3]

Students from developing (largely Commonwealth) countries, were arriving in Britain, hoping to benefit individually and collectively from Western-style higher education. These students had maternalistic expectations of Britain, especially as they had comparable fee and health-care status.[4] However, the reality of their reception has to be placed in the context of the national situation at that time. Britain's shortage of manpower meant that Commonwealth citizens were flocking here to fill unsocial jobs. The indigenous population suddenly saw this influx of immigrants as a threat to their status quo and many overseas people – including students who tended to be classed as immigrants also – had to face racism and prejudice.[5] Studies of the particular problems of student nationality groups at this time included those of Singh[6] on Indian students and Animashawun[7] on African students, whilst Kendall[8] looked specifically at the problems of overseas students and their families at a London college.

Despite the increase in welfare organizations concerned with overseas students, many advisers were seen as being unable to comprehend the problems faced. A lack of rapport with host students, unsuitable accommodation and a failure to be related to as individuals, were all noted as issues in the 1978 study commissioned by the Overseas Students Trust.[9] These issues were raised yet again in this research, based upon Nottingham and Loughborough Universities, as will be described in this chapter.

Pre-arrival information

Overseas students need appropriate, well-timed pre-arrival information in order to alleviate anxieties when facing the unknown. Such communication is a vital prerequisite to a proper understanding of, first, the British culture; second, higher education in general; third, the specific institution at which the student will be working, the institutions' expectations, academic programmes and facilities. This information was found by the research to not always reach students, often due to postal delays and erratic communication services in their home countries. However, departmental recruitment policies also led to delays in sending out this information, which then, due to the overseas countries' communication problems, did not arrive in time.

At Loughborough, when students were offered firm places, the administration sent out 'joining instructions', together with basic information on living in Britain. The crux of pre-arrival uncertainties appeared to be timing; if information was to be better timed the whole admissions process would need to be speeded up.

Some departments and individuals, however, were making efforts to provide pre-arrival support. One department tried to interview potential students in their own country to impart correct information about studying and living in Britain, whilst other departments were found to assume that this information was being sent with the 'joining instructions'. Some tutors sent a personal letter to welcome overseas students, and similarly some hall wardens incorporated this personal touch. The positive effects of such initiatives were thought, by those who practised them, to more than justify the time expended.

Whilst a variety of responses to the overseas students' pre-arrival needs were detected at Loughborough, one area which aroused really strong feelings was that of late recruitment:

> Financial considerations are taking over from common sense. It is not fair to the overseas students or the staff of the department to recruit late just to fill up spaces. Departmental considerations must not be allowed to prevail. We are dealing with people, not pawns! (Central administrator)

Despite the problems which late recruitment presented, a suggestion from the central administration that offers should not be made after 1 September had been regarded by departments as interference:

> Admissions Officers seem determined to maintain their autonomy – largely for financial reasons. (Central administrator)

At Nottingham when a student was offered a firm place at the university, the faculty office was responsible for sending out the offer and accompanying documents, including a leaflet entitled *Information for Overseas Students*. This leaflet gave general information and guidance about the cost of living in England, accommodation, climate and finance. An application form for the one-month preparatory English course together with information about the Welcome Weekend for overseas students, were sent also. This was the only source of information prior to arrival specifically designed for overseas students, until an overseas students prospectus was introduced.

The leaflet *Information for Overseas Students* was produced by a faculty administrator in response to identifying overseas students' needs. The idea was subsequently introduced to other faculties. This innovation was not an initiative of the university administration, but that of an interested individual with no particular brief for this work. Since the leaflet's inception this member of staff remained informally responsible for updating the information, although he felt that it would be a task best performed by a team with different interests and responsibilities for overseas students so that it would remain up-to-date and relevant.

Other documentation sent with the offer varied between departments at Nottingham. Some sent detailed information about the courses the students intended to follow, whereas others provided nothing more than the University prospectus. As a result some students had full information before leaving home about accommodation, course and contacts while others arrived with no idea of where they were to stay and who to contact on arrival.

Whilst all overseas students are susceptible to poor pre-arrival communications, overseas research students have additional problems because they are not joining a specific course, nor are they joining the university at a specific time. Students interviewed for this research expressed a wish to have more information about the direction which their research was to take, together with a checklist of the facilities, both practical and academic, to which they might have access. Information about life in Britain seemed to be particularly erratic, some research students receiving nothing. Where information was received it was thought that this did not acknowledge that they might be mature and have family considerations. Students needed information on the British schooling system (school hours, holidays, how to enrol etc.); nursery provision (cost, hours when available, ages taken, other childminding/creche possibilities etc.); cost-saving shopping possibilities (factory shops, Oxfam and other charity shops, bulk purchase etc.). This information was required well before leaving so that the necessary financial provision could be made, and uncertainties lessened. Above all research students wanted to know where they and their families would live.

Many interviewees said that their main source of information had been an informal network of contacts at home. Because of the weaknesses of existing arrangements and information sources it is recommended that a package of information specifically designed to meet categories of students' (e.g. research) requirements is sent by airmail to reach them before departure, and that these packages should be available at a central point on campus in order to ensure those students who do not receive information prior to their arrival, still have access to it.

First impressions

Some students interviewed for the research criticized the lack of welcome on their arrival, and felt this to be a serious shortcoming, given the problem of culture shock which is experienced in the first crucial weeks of their stay. Appropriate advice and help on arrival are important, since if first impressions are unfavourable the students' whole experience tends to become 'problem'-based.

One female student related her experience of arriving at another university, where initially she was to undertake research. She had arrived there on a cold wet November Sunday. Everywhere was deserted; the key to her room had not been left as promised and there had obviously been a total failure of communications. A porter with a skeleton key was finally found, and he also pointed out the whereabouts of vending machines which were the only source of food and drink. As a new immigrant this student had unfortunately only large denomination money, so her first day was one of coldness, hunger, loneliness and exhaustion. The fact that every detail of this inauspicious arrival was remembered nearly three years later underlines the potency of first impressions. If these are unfavourable, the whole experience may well be viewed in a similar light. Research students are more likely to have such problems because they arrive at unusual times; however, such arrivals are not uncommon when considering overseas students as a whole. Other interviewees mentioned specifically problems with obtaining keys or knowing who to see to get access to their accommodation or even where to find it. One student mentioned arriving at about six on a Saturday evening and being amazed to find shops closed and nowhere being immediately available to buy food.

The research identified an example of good practice, at Nottingham University's School of Education. Students were met at Gatwick Airport and brought by coach to Nottingham. A detailed timetable for the first few weeks was then given to the students so that they knew what to expect. This welcome and timetable provided a feeling of security, especially important when:

> Being in a strange environment makes you lose your confidence. (Overseas student)

However, such provision was not made for many students. Nottingham's *Information for Overseas Students* leaflet made it clear that on arrival students were expected to make their own way to the university. Some universities make arrangements to meet students in London; the British Council meets its own sponsored students who are escorted to their university, and can sometimes make arrangements to meet others. There is recognition of a need to provide a combined university meeting service in October to help students; however, all the help that most Nottingham-bound students received was:

> Emergencies: if you are in difficulties before you arrive in Nottingham you should find the police helpful. Once in Nottingham you should be able to obtain help from the University (N 506101) or the Health Centre (N 501654).

The university switchboard was open twenty-four hours a day but a limited service was provided after six in the evening, when calls were referred to the night security service. The telephone supervisor had no specific instructions concerning queries from arriving students, and referred these to the Overseas Students' Bureau in the Students' Union.

This Overseas Students' Bureau, a Students' Union society run predominantly by second-year students, played a very important part in welcoming new students. As well as manning a telephone in the Students' Union during the arrival period, the bureau members provided a daytime service for newcomers from Nottingham railway station during the first week of term.

There was also a welcome programme for overseas students organized under the supervision of this Overseas Students' Bureau. For many years their welcome consisted of a half-day event organized by the bureau and volunteers from the university staff. This later became a full-day event, but in 1986 the university funded a residential weekend immediately prior to the beginning of the session. This weekend was jointly organized by the bureau and interested university staff, and included help with study skills, university and departmental orientation, practical survival information, a reception attended by the Vice-Chancellor, and a coach tour of Nottingham and its environs.

During the first week of the academic year events were organized by Nottingham Students' Union in order to help students familiarize themselves with the university, and in particular the activities of the union. A package of materials containing details of events, maps, and advertisements for local services such as banks, restaurants and entertainments, was distributed by the Overseas Students' Bureau. The research indicated that not all overseas students received these packages, and that when they did the contents could present a totally bewildering picture of the necessities of student life in Britain.

As with Nottingham, efforts were made at Loughborough to integrate students socially on arrival. The induction evening introduced overseas students to key personnel, and enabled the issuing of information packs. The chaplains and local churches organized 'welcome' evenings, and there was a mayoral reception to link 'town and gown'. The *Students' Union Handbook* detailed societies and clubs, the roles of various executives, and areas specifically useful to overseas students. In addition, an Overseas Student Programme leaflet was placed in key areas of the campus, and the 'Societies Fair' organized through the Students' Union was a means of showing overseas students the various societies and activities available on campus. However, staff wondered whether newly arrived students were ready to make commitments:

> It [the 'Societies Fair'] largely passes overseas students by and could do with being timed later into the term. (Students' Union officer)

Whilst new Nottingham students were provided with a *Student Handbook* which included a small section for overseas students, the most useful publication was provided by the Nottingham Area Council for Overseas Students (NACOSA) through the Overseas Students' Bureau. This gave guidance and information specifically targeted at overseas students on such topics as: study in a foreign country; finance; immigration procedures; illness; transport; shopping; public services; places of interest and useful addresses and telephone numbers.

Hall staff were a further very important part of welcome procedures, and the role of hall porters could be very much overlooked. They played a very valuable role in a student's first anxious moments of arrival after a tiring and maybe frustrating, bewildering journey. The porters' courteous, friendly manner, together with availability and knowledge cannot be overestimated in their importance to the new overseas student.

At Loughborough some of the hall wardens, sub-wardens and supervisors reported feeling less than adequate, particularly if their overseas intake was large. Finding time to help students at the beginning of the academic year was a particular problem.

Catering halls at Loughborough generally organized a formal dinner on the first day of the academic year in order to welcome students and explain the ethos of their hall. One warden emphasized that his hall was a unit, a place to relate to and for two-way communications. However, he was perturbed that if overseas students arrived late, as they often did, then they missed this initiation. Further, wardens of catering halls were found to vary in their desire or ability to mingle with the students:

My predecessor apparently never appeared in the dining hall, but the self-service system gives me a chance to move around and get to know new students. We can also help with such basic uncertainties as which dishes to choose for a 'meal' or which ones conform to religious precepts. We must be immediately aware of dietary problems since these can be very fundamental to success in settling down. (Catering hall warden)

As mentioned above, one of the major problems concerning welcome procedures for overseas students is that these arrangements are usually only available in the first few days of the Autumn term. If there is no one with ongoing responsibility for introducing students who do not arrive at the beginning of the academic year, this presents problems for all of those students whose courses or research do not begin in October or who arrive a few days late. In these situations the onus of providing orientation, information, support and help falls on a variety of people: individual departmental lecturers and supervisors, fellow students and, at Nottingham, the Overseas Students' Bureau.

Interviews with staff at Loughborough University confirmed the need for students to feel really welcome, and staff were conscious of this as they assessed the provision made:

The actual procedure is weak. On the crucial arrival weekend, the Accommodation Office stays open but other areas which could help – such as food supplies, advice – do not. Overseas students appear to arrive with very little on the Saturday or Sunday yet, by Monday they must be in their departments to register. The campus is vast. There is no central information bureau, no hall porters. Nothing is staffed twenty-four hours a day.

Students do arrive at all hours because, having crossed time zones and some having already experienced traumatic bureaucratic procedures on entry, they just want to get here. Security staff just might pick them up. (Residential Organisation representative)

Overseas students arriving thus were likely to suffer disorientation and culture shock of the most immediate kind, connected as they are with the actual processes of living. In order to overcome this problem the Student Counselling Service at Loughborough, amongst others, discerned the need for a two- or three-day compulsory orientation course immediately prior to the academic year.

Whilst the Student Counsellors considered that this would be cost-effective in the long term they expected adverse reaction from those involved in halls and catering, whose finances would be more directly and measurably affected by such a programme in the short term.

All overseas students arriving at Loughborough on the appointed days were met by home students at the railway station or coach stop. However, there was no evidence of volunteer peer-pairing, which has been employed successfully on some other British campuses.

The *Student Manual* at Loughborough designated the Student Record Office as the first point of contact for all new overseas students to make enquiries, and the secretarial staff found themselves overwhelmed by them in the early days of the academic year. These staff had not received training in, for example, defusing 'incidents' but, with experience had evolved their own style:

I try to maintain a steady insistence on ways of proceeding here whilst recognizing the early difficulties experienced by some cultures in accepting these. (Secretary, Student Record Office)

As with Nottingham, departments at Loughborough were found to make varying efforts to admit and welcome new overseas students. One department thought social interaction between students very important and introduced new students to their fellow countrymen and -women who were already students in the department. This was found to be very reassuring to new students. Some departments introduced overseas students either socially or formally to academics, other staff who might assist them, or to fellow researchers. Some students received an initial briefing from their personal tutor.

One department, with a long record of handling overseas students in large numbers, had evolved its own arrival procedures. Time and place of arrival were advised in good time and students arriving more than one week late were not admitted. On arrival, students found staff who were familiar with their home situation and a departmental programme of introductions and social events which involved virtually all staff. The first week was regarded as an introductory one, with orientation to the department, the campus, town and local area, all undertaken by the department.

On both campuses during the period of the research there was evidence of much goodwill being exercised by all categories of staff, in order to smooth the path of new, possibly disoriented students. However, with large numbers of students overall, and personnel under pressure, there was a feeling that staff might be failing their overseas students just when they were most needed. UKCOSA has urged comprehensive orientation programmes and adequate staff training as ways of ensuring that overseas students have a smooth arrival, and the reactions of Loughborough staff, at least partially, endorsed this view:

> It is imperative to get the first three weeks right. Overseas students need to feel settled in every aspect of their personal lives if they are to have a chance of developing fully as true students. (Course tutor)

Accommodation

Good accommodation in a comfortable and relaxing environment is an important prerequisite for settling down to study. This is particularly important for overseas students because their accommodation will be their home during their studies.

The research demonstrated that a large number of students surveyed experienced some difficulties with accommodation, and that these had adversely affected their ability to settle to their work. Research students in particular experienced difficulties often aggravated by their characteristics – mature and often married with families – and the time they spent at the university. Students reported that problems and worries over accommodation, compounded by indifferent attitudes from university staff, were counter-productive to motivation and could induce depression.

Prior to setting off for their stay at a university abroad, prospective students require adequate information on the availability of accommodation and its cost. The research found that many students reached near panic over the lack of accommodation information and confirmation. The British Council recognized the problem faced by these students and regretted that it could be prevented from trying to overcome this:

> Pre-arranged accommodation is the axis of students' ability to feel catered for and settled. They can then cope with other unknowns. We are particularly disappointed that we cannot block book accommodation since charges are always paid in advance and our students very rarely drop out once accepted. (British Council representative)

The two prime causes of the problems faced by students at this stage were problems with mail deliveries overseas, and departments making last-minute offers to students. The situation at Nottingham illustrates the latter: by 1 August requests for accommodation were confirmed and places in hall guaranteed; however, thereafter no guarantee could be given.

But because of mail delays information concerning accommodation did not always reach students. One of the surveys at Loughborough found that twenty-three per cent had received no information on accommodation prior to their arrival. It was also found that a significant number of students at both universities arrived from overseas expecting accommodation and finding none. Many overseas students may assume that the offer of a place automatically means the provision of accommodation and this leads to an additional burden for those responsible for accommodation arrangements:

> Sorting out accommodation for those students without concrete arrangements produces tremendous overload. Some really do expect it to be part of their acceptance package. We experience many hassles from overseas students but we have to cope with the actual. For example, if a student turns up with a family and nowhere to live we cannot just abandon them. We have got to act humanely. (Residential Organisation representative.)

Whilst some universities give priority to overseas students having accommodation on campus, this was not the case with the institutions in this study. Allocation to halls of residence tended to be arbitrary, the aim being to mix students to provide a feeling of internationalism. Opinions differed as to whether this was necessarily the most appropriate action. At Nottingham it has been suggested that there should be an international hall, bringing together all overseas students. Some groups preferred to live together, where their specific need of accommodation during vacations could be met, and the problem of catering for different diets could be eased. However, there were those who felt that this would unsatisfactorily isolate overseas students from the remainder of the student body.

When lists of students were received by hall wardens it was not always possible to discern their nationalities or sex. Hence it was difficult to accurately pair and group students. For example, at Loughborough, where female students were heavily outnumbered by males, wardens insisted on women students, including those from overseas, being placed in sufficiently large numbers to enable them to relate socially. Due to inadequate information initial room allocations might not prove satisfactory: however, the special requirements of overseas students were given sympathetic consideration when this occurred; for instance, Iranian students wary of one another and not wishing to share. This could also be true of Nigerian students from different tribes.

Overseas students from affluent backgrounds found facilities on campus very basic, and were sometimes thought to be imperious in their demands of residential staff. Hall supervisors were often the staff who received these complaints.

At Nottingham University some overseas students had difficulty in appreciating the hall philosophy of communality and sharing, together with the idea of the study–bedroom as a private area used to work in as well as for living and sleeping. Mature students also had difficulty in acclimatizing to hall life. They could find it noisy and disturbing.

Despite these problems the research identified many wardens taking special pains to help overseas students to adjust to their university environment. In one hall it was noted that the cleaners made a point of knocking on every door each day, and proved excellent in perceiving overseas students' needs, helping with their washing and offering a sympathetic ear.

Unfortunately, however great individual efforts are, wider issues can hinder overseas students feeling at home:

> Financial considerations always have to predominate. Nothing can run at a loss so there is no leeway for special requests such as overseas students wanting to organize a national celebration meal. (Hall warden.)

It was not unusual to find that when students were housed on campus they had to leave their accommodation during the summer months. At Nottingham students had to seek alternative off-campus accommodation during the summer, whilst at Loughborough most students in catering halls had to move to self-catering campus accommodation each vacation. Such movement was disruptive to the students concerned.

The Residential Organisation was, however, faced with a serious problem:

> If we put all overseas students into one or two Halls, we should be accused of discrimination. We aim to spread them. Nor could we keep all Halls open during the vacations for very small numbers of students. Conferences have to be held in the same accommodation to make the Hall pay. (Residential Organisation representative)

Trying to meet the needs of overseas students, and ensure that accommodation is 'paying its way' through being available for meetings, conferences and so on, presented a difficult conflict for staff concerned. Since 1986 overseas undergraduates at Nottingham had been allowed to stay in their halls, although not necessarily in their own rooms, and they had to make their own arrangements for meals. Obviously this was only a partial solution.

Postgraduate students at both universities, but particularly at Nottingham which had only seventy self-contained postgraduate flats, and some for undergraduates from overseas, found that they had to seek accommodation off-campus. Generally this was not welcome for a number of reasons.

Off-campus accommodation was not arranged until students had arrived on campus, to ensure personal contact between the student and the property owner. This usually necessitated the student staying in a hotel or other similar temporary lodgings. The effect of public exposure to cultural and dietary differences, together with the adverse effects of transiency could create significant problems here. Residing in temporary accommodation might persist for some time; students surveyed spoke of several weeks and even three months. Too many students appeared to spend their early days this way, providing an unnecessary hurdle during the crucial first term, so much a key to the success of the overseas student's stay.

Students seeking off-campus accommodation reported receiving little help from the residential organizations, often having to make their own arrangements through estate agents. Loughborough students found the size of this small market town a problem, together with the age and substandard nature of its housing for rent, unscrupulous landlords and covert colour bars. In fact, the latter was mentioned by students from both universities, reporting that they were subject to racial prejudice when seeking accommodation.

Living off-campus, once accommodation had been found, was by no means trouble-free either. Students reported finding running costs for their new homes, especially heating, very expensive and above their expectations. There was a problem of travelling distances to their universities, particularly when they had no car. Distance also created a reluctance to return to campus in the evening, which restricted students' use of university facilities and opportunities to mix socially with British students: this led to feelings of isolation.

The students surveyed expected guidance and advice when seeking off-campus accommodation, and some university staff suggested that these students needed as much support as 'freshers'. Some students felt that when providing campus accommodation preference should in fact be given to over-seas students, because of their difficulties in coping well with the situation and the attitudes of the general community. However, the residential organizations found that the recruitment policies of departments made assured places for overseas students in campus accommodation impossible:

> We can only issue specific accommodation to a named student. Depart-ments and admission tutors do not start early enough with their offers. Departmental quotas are based on the previous year's take-up, which may poorly indicate actual need. Heads of departments must be made aware of the consequences of tardy admissions policies. (Residential Organisation representative)

Some efforts were being made, however, to assist with finding off-campus accommodation. Nottingham made a minibus available so that overseas students could be driven to look at privately rented accommodation, and Loughborough maintained a list of property available, and stated minimum requirements for furnishing, heating, bathroom and kitchen facilities.

A large proportion of the students surveyed were married and had families, and many of these wished to have their partners and families accompany them to Britain, especially research students who would be resident for more than one year. However, both universities advised against this due to a lack of suitable accommodation. Despite this warning, many students ignored this advice, and some of these then felt reluctant to seek advice and floundered in making their own arrangements.

Apart from the natural inclination not to be parted from partners and children, overseas students have other reasons for ignoring the universities' guidance, for example, in some countries it is not socially acceptable to leave one's family. Some male students found that they had difficulty in catering for themselves and had sent for their families so that their wives could undertake the time-consuming domestic chores.

Families seeking campus accommodation found no such provision at Lough-borough, and limited provision at Nottingham. Seeking off-campus accom-modation presented the same problems as experienced by single overseas students: poor standards of housing, distance, prejudice and so on. Once settled, problems continued. Wives were lonely and isolated, often with no English, and with young children obstructing the opportunity to learn. Male

students found themselves solely responsible for shopping, overseeing schooling, rent arrangements, transport, medical matters and similar, all interfering
with studies. If on-campus housing could be provided, families of similar
culture groups could be together, and mutual support, help and friendship
could help to overcome these problems.

Despite the apparent need for suitable accommodation at Loughborough:

> The Residential Organisation has no plans to provide university-owned
> family accommodation on or off campus. (Welfare Organiser)

even though:

> Indifferent accommodation, cold weather, inability to speak English
> and no employment prospects – lead to social isolation of the spouse.
> (Residential Organisation)

Nottingham University equally did not believe that it had any responsibility
for providing family accommodation, and was selling that which it owned on the
edge of its campus: these houses were seen to be a drain on resources and capital
as they needed renovation. Several students surveyed, however, referred to
overseas students opting for similar courses at other universities solely because
of the problems of finding suitable family accommodation.

Relationships with the Residential Organisation were not always very satisfactory, and in fact one of the fears expressed by an overseas postgraduate
student was 'treatment at the Accommodation Office'. The insecurity experienced by the newly arrived overseas student sometimes produced an aggressive
attitude to staff, and frustration with the unfamiliar queueing system could lead
to eruptions of temper. Mainly staffed by women, it was not unusual to find
some male students, due to their cultural background, treating those working
for the Residential Organisation as inferior. Cultural differences also led to
some students exhibiting bribe and barter behaviour, which were frowned upon
by staff concerned.

Despite these problems, and lack of training in personal relationships, the
university staff concerned felt confident that they had evolved coping strategies.
Those at the centre of the Residential Organisation had to maintain a viable
system, whilst those continually in contact with students had to be mindful of
their personal welfare. Sometimes this was found to cause conflict which called
upon the skills of all concerned. Another difficulty faced by staff was the severe
overloading at the beginning of term, especially the first of an academic year,
which resulted in a lack of time and inclination to look at problems in detail.
Obviously, despite coping strategies, the system was working against staff
fulfilling their role adequately and yet:

> If overseas students are happy in their residential situation they will act as
> ambassadors . . . on their return home. (Hall warden)

What sort of an ambassador is this student likely to be?

> Despite all that has happened since, I shall never forget the chaos of those
> first few days! (Overseas student)

The surveys of overseas students at both universities evolved a consensus of opinion as to their accommodation requirements. Initially, accurate information on accommodation is required prior to arrival. Understandably students do not like setting out to a foreign country without knowing where they are to live. Campus accommodation is much preferred, and there are expectations that the offer of a university place should imply the provision of suitable campus accommodation. This provision should include facilities for families. Students seek adequately equipped permanent accommodation, where they will be able to relax and feel 'at home' both during term and vacation times.

Where it proves impossible to provide campus accommodation, it is felt that suitable arrangements should be made for students prior to their arrival, and the use of temporary accommodation be discontinued.

Food

Whilst some overseas students come to accept university catering arrangements quite quickly, others find some fundamental difficulties. Newly arrived students even expressed deep concerns as to whether they would be able to cope with the British diet without becoming unhealthy:

> The diet in England is quite different from the one in Hong Kong. I am afraid that I will get very fat. (Overseas student)

Indeed some overseas students anticipate that food is going to be a major problem to them, and pre-arrival information explaining British eating habits and describing British food would help here.

Efforts were being made to take into consideration overseas students' dietary needs, with regular vegetarian meals and rice being on offer in halls of residence. At Loughborough during Ramadan one dining room remained open until late. However, halal or ritually slaughtered meat is not available, though some hall dining-room supervisors tried to be on hand so that suitable alternative foods could be recommended. Nottingham's catering staff was also sensitive to overseas students' needs, but special foods and diets mean extra costs, and decisions to provide these have to be based on economic considerations.

Students in self-catering accommodation were able to prepare their own national dishes, but where kitchens had to be shared problems occurred, for example, use of cooking equipment by Muslim and non-Muslim students, and a dislike of different cooking habits. Chinese students like to cater in bulk, which can provide difficulties, not least to the cleaners of the kitchen being used.

Climate

Britain's climate was found to be a cause of concern for some overseas students. They worried about coping with long, cold winters, and where they were living in off-campus accommodation heating bills produced another problem. It was found that students tended to underestimate the amount they would have to spend on heating and warm clothing.

Wardens at both universities had identified the heating needs of overseas students. Those interviewed at Nottingham suggested that higher levels of heating were necessary, and at Loughborough a less rigid approach to seasonal heating was introduced. Overseas students were seen to become miserable in the cold, damp conditions of the British winter, and the absence of sunshine also had an effect on their spirits. A warm room in which to study, relax and sleep can help to redress the balance here.

There is a requirement for pre-arrival information on the climate and the cost of heating, together with advice on the type of clothing to purchase and how to wear it to ensure warmth, for example, the wearing of layers of clothing and a hat or similar, the purchase of boots rather than shoes, and the necessity of having gloves. If possible, guidance on where such clothing can be purchased at reasonable cost should be included.

Money

An area of concern for many overseas students was the cost of living in Britain, although this greatly depended upon the student's home country. In particular they felt unprepared for the high cost of housing, heating and warm clothing, and considered that more helpful pre-course information should be provided to prepare them for this expenditure.

Even so forewarned, however, the overseas student's financial security is often threatened by the changing political and economic fortunes of either the family or country supporting his or her studies. Whilst meeting the cost of living presents a cause for stress and worry, students can find themselves with additional financial concerns because their fees have not been paid. Overseas students' fees are paid by a variety of sources, not all of which are reliable. Some universities have financial penalties for late payment, and a good deal of time is employed in chasing fees. The Student Finance Officer at Nottingham travelled to London just before graduation each year in order to extract fees due from embassies, so that worried students could graduate.

When settling fees some students have found problems with negotiation of exchange control, cheque clearance and frequent visits to the Finance Office, all time-consuming and in some cases humiliating. Where it is possible to pay fees by instalment, or to have an extension for payment of fees, these are welcomed.

Both academic staff and those in the Student Finance Office found themselves involved with these problems. The tendency was for the academic staff to be helping students with extra special financial problems, whilst the Student Finance Officer would be dealing with day-to-day problems, which could be very time-consuming.

Where students are responsible for paying their own fees and expenses, they are considerably affected by rising costs, which bring their own worries, as well as putting increased pressure upon these students to succeed. UKCOSA has highlighted the many financial pitfalls these students can experience, and urged universities to carefully consider their policies towards overseas students' financial problems.

Pastoral care

The presence of overseas students on a university campus was considered by those interviewed for this research to require increased provisions of personal counselling, financial assistance, complex rights and welfare advice, and possible extra demands upon medical and other welfare services:

> The hierarchy is slowly coming to the view that overseas students need specific support arrangements which, in some cases, differ from the needs of home students. Rapport between welfarers and policy makers is increasing. Welfarers do have a say and some relationships are building up.

Attention has already been drawn to the pastoral role of wardens of halls of residence. Others concerned with student pastoral care include the following:

Departmental administrators

These staff are a very important area of non-academic support to overseas students. Although answerable to their departments, their liaison with central administration was found to be generally good. They were found also to be prepared to deal with all kinds of requests made by overseas students, and took a very personal interest in their welfare:

> Students talk to us because they have to be here in the department so this makes it easier. We keep an eye on them and refer them to other sources of help since tutors vary in their capacity to respond or take an interest in their needs. (Departmental administrator)

Finance Officer

As already mentioned, students with financial queries or problems were referred to the Finance Officer. The problems often occurred due to actions of home governments or bureaucratic delays, and these were reported as sympathetically handled. However, the Finance Officer at Loughborough also quoted instances where students had tried to take advantage of this department's sympathetic arrangements, and these had to be vigilantly spotted.

Despite this, many cases of genuine hardship presented themselves to this officer. Sometimes students lived beyond their means and entered into financial difficulties which required financial counselling.

Student counsellors

At Loughborough the main thrust of the Counselling Service's work was in counselling students on a wide variety of individual issues. With a very small staff, the service found itself fully stretched, and the Overseas Student Programme it provided had to be somewhat peripheral. This programme took the form of several formal occasions spread through the year to make overseas students feel important and valued, and a series of workshops including orientation, study skills, re-orientation and social integration.

About thirty-five per cent of the total case work at Loughbourgh was thought to be with overseas students – a figure disproportionately high in relation to the overall percentage of students from overseas. A similar finding came from statistics compiled by the Counselling Service at Nottingham. These figures have to be taken in the context of cultural differences which mean that students from many countries cannot countenance the suggestion that they are not coping.

The problems presented by overseas students were found to differ very little from those of home students, but it could be said that when they suffer problems overseas students tend to do so more intensely. Several areas of problems were particularly noted.

- Anxieties about being rejected and left out, sometimes associated with being foreign and with language difficulties.
- Striving for perfection.
- Flight from relationship problems and resulting anxieties and guilt feelings.

The work of the student counsellors was made more difficult by overseas students seeming to expect solutions, and their disillusionment when these are not immediately forthcoming. It seemed to be more difficult to inculcate an understanding that the counsellor's role is one of helper and enabler rather than one of adviser and problem solver. A further barrier to the effectiveness of the Counselling Service was the perception of some overseas students that the service was purely associated with problems rather than with the development of positive coping strategies.

Student Union Welfare Adviser

Students with queries relating to status, visas, or nationality, or with problems on fixing rents or dealing with landlords, could be referred to the Rights and Welfare Adviser operating from the Students' Union. The experience of the adviser at Nottingham was that enquiries from overseas students could be very complex, and often they had to be referred to other, more specialist, agencies. This adviser also received referrals from the university administration; an enquiry from a prospective postgraduate about schooling for his children was cited as an example.

Health officers

At Nottingham a series of studies was undertaken between 1968 and 1973 which demonstrated that higher demands on the Health Centre were made by overseas students. The head of the centre reported that the needs of overseas students differed from those of home students in a variety of ways, all of which contributed to this higher demand:

- Overseas students have no conception of how to use the National Health Service. In most countries people go straight to hospital so the idea of lengthy referrals through the GP is a new process which has to be explained. Much time is spent on educating students on how the system works in England.
- No previous health records are available so there are problems of diagnosis when no background is known.
- As a result of changes in climate and exposure to new kinds of viruses in England overseas students suffer common cold and other minor (to British people) illnesses to which they have no immunity.
- The incidence of psychological problems presented is no different than those presented by home students, but where these arise they tend to take a more severe and dramatic form and pose extra problems of interpretation for the staff. The pressures on overseas students to succeed are regarded as being responsible for extreme reactions to stress such as breakdown and, on occasion, suicide.
- Mature students coming with families with the varying needs of the whole family to be catered for, especially since postgraduates often see this as a good time to have children.
- Unrealistic expectations of the service in expecting long-standing illnesses to be cured.
- Importation of diseases such as TB and Hepatitis B which have not been a problem in Britain in recent years.

Alongside the Nottingham Health Centre, a ward for in-patient care was provided for students. This was particularly important for students who lived on campus because they were not permitted to remain in hall when they had an infectious disease or a long illness. A fee of £6 per annum was charged to all students who registered for this facility, but the fee was subject to objection by the Students' Union on the basis that such provision should be made by the university free of charge and they discouraged students from paying it. From the point of view of the overseas student there was an important disadvantage of the in-patient care in that it did not cater for vacation periods. On the whole this had not been a problem as it had always been possible to make other arrangements for the occasional student who was ill during this period by, for example, moving into the hall warden's or a friend's house but no one was satisfied with such arrangements and there were fears that increasing numbers of overseas students could cause the breakdown of goodwill gestures of this kind.

Some students tended to come to the doctor with trivial queries that would be better handled by the health visitor or the district nurse, as they saw only the doctor as the resource for their health problems and did not understand the function of other parts of the community nursing provision. Medical staff at Loughborough had noticed that overseas students wanted to relate to one person at the medical centre. They could not recognize the role of nurses and assistants, even if they were the most appropriate personnel to see.

Health staff at Loughborough thought it essential to liaise with other areas of expertise on campus so that all facets of a problem could be reviewed. Some interviewees also considered that there was some deficiency in the communication channels between departments and the health centre when students became ill.

British Council officers

The British Council has a wide-ranging commitment to its students, providing on-going support. Queries and problems are followed up with departments, halls of residence, embassies and other bodies as necessary. Due to the Council's presence in many overseas countries, students seemed able to relate easily to its image in Britain. With regular payments, accommodation arrangements and support, all provided or arranged by the British Council, students gained confidence and seemed to have few real problems. Other students had to go to many different supporting agencies to obtain the same level of help, and even then had to cope with the actual administration themselves.

Chaplains

Christian overseas students were found to have special expectations of university life and they had to come to terms with the reality:

> Overseas students assume that a Christian presence will be felt on campus.
> The notion of a secular institution is somewhat alien to them. (Chaplain)

Apart from supporting students and trying to make them feel part of a family, the chaplains aimed to offer practical help when genuine need arose, without bureaucracy or formality. Clothing, travel facilities and small loans featured quite frequently here. However, one chaplain was quite firm in the view that the university had obligations to overseas students:

> It should provide a properly resourced structure in return for their cheques. Charitable acts should not be the basis of assistance.

The chaplains were also concerned about the familial responsibilities of overseas students, particularly their extended family ties.

Faculty Adviser for Overseas Students

In recognition of the special needs for information and advice that overseas students have from time to time, in 1979 Nottingham University Senate established an adviser for each faculty. Advisers were selected from academic staff but no extra remuneration was attached to the role. The original intention was that tutors deal with their own students generally and only refer to the Faculty Adviser in difficult cases. In some faculties this seemed to be the practice but in others it was said that some tutors thought that all overseas students' problems should go straight to the adviser. In practice it seemed that Faculty Advisers received few referrals but where they were referred the problems could be very complex and time-consuming. Issues tended to concern financial difficulties such as getting foreign exchange approval from the student's own country, liaising with other governments over funds, tapping educational funds for help, negotiating bank loans and so on, or issues concerning immigration, visas and other problems concerning political status. One of the dilemmas facing the Faculty Advisers was that in order to be effective they had to keep abreast of the mass of ever-changing regulations and conditions affecting overseas students in respect of finance and immigration in particular and yet, since the job carried no time allocation, no funding of any kind, and no training, it was difficult to justify such a potentially high input of time for learning these matters for the sake of the few referrals the Faculty Adviser might have each year. Faculty Advisers thought the arrangements were unsatisfactory, both to students and advisers.

The idea of a central source of information which advisers could contact was favoured, but others felt that the whole role was an anomaly and served little purpose and should be abandoned in favour of departmental advisers who could link into a central co-ordinator providing specialist knowledge. Difficulties in finding staff willing to take on this task in the Science Faculty in 1985 resulted in an adviser being appointed for each department within the faculty, and this pattern was being considered in other faculties, but this development did not address the question of the role of the adviser and the problem of the complexity of the knowledge needed to be able to help with a variety of problem areas. Some argued that such a development might be counter-productive and simply result in overseas students being referred to a person seen as their adviser for all problems instead of encouraging students to learn how to use the general support facilities provided on campus.

Students interviewed expressed regret at the loss of valuable time in finding advice and aid from the appropriate agency. In the United States the support and socialization of overseas students is very professionally treated and also well co-ordinated.[10] It was this co-ordination which tended to be found lacking at Loughborough and Nottingham, despite individual initiatives. There was a strong case for a central bureau for overseas students with a co-ordinator who could provide a permanent base for the mass of relevant information. This person could also be responsible for developing and maintaining a range of facilities from pre-arrival information to welcome and social arrangements. Such a bureau would require permanent staff with the knowledge, skills, experience and maturity required for meeting the varied needs of overseas students.

Many universities already provide a specialist overseas students service and since the evidence suggests that overseas students when choosing a university are now interested in the support facilities available to them, as well as the quality of course offered, provision of such a bureau would be attractive as well as beneficial to them.

Socialization

As mentioned in the section concerning welcoming procedures, efforts were made to inform overseas students of facilities, societies and the like available to them on campus at both universities. It is important that all students take time off for relaxation, and this was recognized by respondents in this research. However, not only is relaxation important to the general well-being of the student, it can be a useful way of overcoming feelings of homesickness and loneliness.

Hall wardens were found to accept the need to be vigilant for homesickness, withdrawal and the inability to cope socially. Mature students were as much in need of this concern as their younger colleagues.

In a letter issued during the span of this research to all new students, the Vice-Chancellor at Loughborough recommended seeking:

> . . . to balance study and play in a sensible way . . . take advantage of all the University has to offer by way of extra-curricular activities, be it sport, community involvement or societies.

This exhortation to all was taken by many overseas students to be an open invitation to social involvement. Unfortunately the reality was found by many to be rather different. For some students, language proved to be a barrier, because speech hesitancy constrained efforts to be sociable when they first arrived. Without the ability to communicate freely and confidently, it was a great temptation to seek socialization in national groups. If this occurred and friendships were established, it was found that there was less tendency to break into a British group. Hence, as several interviewees explained, provision of opportunities and the ability to seize them did not necessarily equate.

Within the hall organization at Loughborough, wardens interviewed said that they had come to realize that it was up to them to guide their social committees toward recognizing the needs of overseas students. Wardens also drew attention to the fact that overseas students were often very involved with their own societies and groups. These were highly organized and affiliated in many cases to groups in other parts of the country, for example, the Pakistani five-a-side league. Students might hold high office in these societies but this was not always known by the wardens.

Representation of overseas students on hall committees was found to be disproportionately low at Loughborough and Nottingham. Only in one hall, where overseas students formed a high percentage of the residents, were they well represented. The socializing of home and overseas students in halls was considered very variable.

Overseas students housed off-campus at Loughborough were assigned to a hall; however, this did not produce instant friendships and many overseas students here without their families were considered to be very lonely, and looked elsewhere for social provision:

> These students spend their own time not only off-campus but often away from Loughborough. There is no actual exclusion of overseas students but as soon as lectures are over the social lives of overseas and home students tend not to come together. (Personal tutor)

If off-campus students were living with their families, a further barrier to socialization was sometimes found to be erected.

Loughborough departmental efforts to provide a social context were extremely variable; some did not see it as part of their role at all. Some confined socializing to welcoming students at the beginning of the academic year. This was particularly unfortunate for research students, many of whom needed departmental socialization to redress the balance of academic isolation. Only one or two departments appeared to have ongoing social programmes. These worked on the rationale that all groups included a spokesperson who would convey what was wanted and appropriate gatherings were then organized. These departments made a conscious effort to include the families of their overseas students and the participation of academic staff gave credence to the ethos of shared experiences in all the activities of a department.

The various national societies at Loughborough and Nottingham were affiliated to the Students' Union, and received a share of Union funds. Many of these were found to be flourishing during the period of the research, particularly when it came to celebrating national festivals and feasts. However, due to difficulties with catering, these societies often held their events off campus. The Students' Union and its buildings were found to be under-used by overseas and home students:

> There is almost total desolation in the Union building after 7.00 pm apart from the bar. We have to convince overseas students that we have more to offer than this. (Students' Union officer)

The Overseas Students' Bureau was a particular feature of Nottingham's Students' Union. Unlike the other Union national societies which made a direct appeal to students from particular countries, the Bureau attracted all overseas students. The Bureau organized social activities for its members and tried to attract home students to its activities to present a truly international atmosphere of interchange, rather than being a club which isolated overseas students. Like other student societies the Bureau was run by students and there were no full-time officers. Its main limitation was that since the officers changed each year and were usually second-year undergraduates, the Bureau had little expertise to bring to the work. To help overcome this problem of discontinuity, some members of the university staff who were interested in the Bureau's work attended meetings.

The International Festival which was organized by the Overseas Students' Association at Loughborough had been successful in drawing interested people to the Union Building to experience a little of the multi-cultural nature of the

chaplain as an intermediary, probably because of social uncertainties. Suggestions by the chaplains for liaison with British students and off-campus families had been received enthusiastically but, in the event, it was the overseas students who did not participate. Offers to 'have a student for Christmas' were not always taken up either.

It was not often clear what kind of adjustments students would have to make to the British culture and ways of behaving, however some students did specify the irritation they felt at the slow pace of life, and the time wasted due to the inconvenience of shopping hours. The peace of England compared with the noise of Hong Kong was mentioned as a problem:

> The most difficult problem to me is the silent environment. I feel lonely and frightened in such an environment.

On the other hand students welcomed the relatively peaceful and relaxed way of life:

> In England the people work slowly and the attitude to others is kind and reachable. Even the bus drivers are smiling to each commuter . . .
>
> People in England are very polite . . . sometimes when I go to the market I find that even the hawkers are polite.

Unfortunately not all students had been so fortunate in their contact with local people, bad experiences being usually due to racial prejudice. However, there was a general desire amongst students to make the most of their stay in Britain. One student summed up the fairly ambivalent feelings of most of the students when he said:

> I am used to living as part of a majority. Being in the minority will require adjustments. I look forward to it because so far a good number of people seem friendly. Some people however give me uncomfortable looks.

The students interviewed were aware that living in Britain would often require a change in their life-style, referring to such things as socializing, particularly if they did not like the atmosphere in pubs and bars. Most accepted the need to adjust but the spirit with which adjustment would be made varied:

> I come from a culture different in everything from Britain, therefore I have to adapt myself to living here and to contact with the society, and to be like the others because I have to change myself and my ideas as I can – but that does not mean that I forget my culture and personal characteristics.

Amongst the most reluctant to accept change were three Japanese students:

> I am not English, I am willing to take some English idea if I think it wonderful . . . However, I would like to keep my Japanese way of life as I am not sure this change would be acceptable in Japan . . .
>
> I will make personal adjustment superficially to get along with people. But I always want to be conscious about the difference and try to keep my Japanese personality because Western way of thinking is not accepted in Japan yet.

I don't really like to change myself for the English life-style ... my characteristic personality has been completed already by receiving the education.

Whilst respecting these views, one wonders how far the fear of losing one's own national identity could prohibit socialization, and the benefits this could bring, with students from other national groups.

Conclusion

The experiences of overseas students in Britain are not confined to their academic studies. They also have to live within their host country, and the more satisfactorily their living needs are met, the more likely their success in their academic endeavours.

From this chapter it is clear that students covered by the research expressed concerns beginning with the lack or inadequacy of pre-arrival information, unfortunate first impressions, leading on to accommodation problems, difficulties with money, food, the climate and socializing, and the identification of information agencies. Not all students suffered from all of these problems, but usually they had experienced one if not several.

If universities maintain their interest in recruiting students from abroad it is obvious that they must also recognize the financial and organizational implications for ensuring that these students are adequately catered for in all of these areas, and that they return home having enjoyed both studying and living in this country.

References

1. F. Dunlop, *Europe's Guests, Students and Trainees: a Survey on the Welfare of Foreign Students and Trainees in Europe*. Strasbourg, Council for Cultural Co-operation of the Council of Europe, 1966.
2. Sir W. Lee-Warner, *Report of the Committee on Indian Students Part 2: Evidence*, London, HMSO for the India Office, 1922.
3. G. Banjo, 'Cultural castration', *UKCOSA News*, 7 (1975), 14–18, is one example of such a study.
4. Political and Economic Planning, 'Students from the colonies', *Planning*, 20 (1954), 374.
5. Political and Economic Planning. *New Commonwealth Students in Britain*, London, Political and Economic Planning, 1965.
6. A. Singh, *Indian Students in Britain*, London, Asia Publishing House, 1963.
7. G. Animashawun, 'African students in Britain', *Race*, 5 (1963), 38–47.
8. M. Kendall, *Overseas Students and their Families: a Study at a London College*, London, Research Unit for Students' Problems, 1968.
9. B. Reed, J. Hutton and J. Bazalgette, *Freedom to Study. Requirements of Overseas Students in the UK*, London, Overseas Students Trust, 1978.
10. H. M. Jenkins, *Educating Students from Other Nations*, San Francisco, Jossey-Bass, 1983.

5

Staff Development and Training

John Barker

The purpose of this chapter is to examine the part which staff training and development can play in achieving the objective of providing overseas students with the learning opportunities, associated facilities, pastoral care and back-up services which they have the right to expect from their institutions.

From the beginning, the reader needs to be aware of the perspective. The material contained in this chapter is based on the research carried out at two universities, to which the author has added his own experience gained in twenty years' involvement in training in a wide variety of organizations. Other educational institutions may face different or additional problems, may be further or less far along the road towards developing a coherent policy in regard to overseas students and a systematic programme of staff training and develop-ment within that policy. It is essential for institutions to conduct their own analyses. This chapter may serve as a starting point.

At this early stage the issue in question, staff training and development, must also be put into context. As long ago as 1969, Talbot and Ellis wrote, 'Training for the sake of particular individuals or groups or, worse still, for its own sake, only militates against the main purpose of training for the sake of the operation.'[1] We should train to meet specifically identified needs and those needs should be closely linked to the objectives of the organization, short and long term. In the case of overseas students, therefore, the institution has to ask itself first of all why it wants to recruit them and, having answered that question honestly, proceed to developing its operational plan, an integral part of which is the training and development of its staff to carry out effectively the functions which the plan requires. This might be called a 'target shooting' approach. The alternative is the 'shotgun' approach, whereby as much training as possible is 'loaded up' and pointed in roughly the right direction: some of it, hopefully, is bound to hit the target. Training, however, takes time and costs money and it may well be that time and money could have been spent to greater effect somewhere else within the institution.[2] Moreover, with this approach we may actually do more harm than good. Training means change. After an effective piece of training, people have been changed at least to the extent that they now possess new knowledge or skills, the desire to use the knowledge and skills and the expectation that they will have opportunities to do so and receive recognition from the organization in some form or other for this. Yet, if the training, however good, is not the direct response to an identified developmental need, which itself has been created by the requirements of an operational plan, the likelihood is that nothing else has changed except for the trainees. There are no further resources; there is still no recognition for their efforts; the same inadequate systems continue. In the face of such organizational indifference, the consequences so often are disappointment, frustration, hostility, and a loss of motivation. It is in this light that the question of staff training and development should be viewed.

The research project did not set out to be specifically an analysis of training needs. It was an investigation into the experiences of overseas students living and working at two universities. What it did uncover was a considerable number of operational problems and difficulties on the part of both students and staff. These problems afford the most immediate and obvious point of entry for the reader into the process of identifying training needs and specifying training solutions, although to do this involves at this stage some distortion of the systematic approach to training needs analysis, which requires us to start with organizational objectives. It will therefore be necessary to step back a little later on.

The wide variety of operational problems and difficulties has already been described in detail elsewhere but in order to derive from them a coherent statement of training needs and an achievable programme of training to match, they need to be refined down according to their common elements into a more manageable number of categories. Taking the students' viewpoint first, the difficulties appear to fall largely into the following categories: those encountered in the process of learning; those encountered in the process of interacting with staff; feelings of uncertainty and confusion; feelings of insecurity and inferiority; pre-arrival communications; information and advice at point of arrival; accommodation; social interaction; and cultural, dietary and climatic change. The difficulties encountered by staff can be grouped together as follows: those deriving from university policies; those deriving from university systems; those arising from perceived university attitudes towards teaching and tutoring; uncertainty about certain roles; negative attitudes on the part of staff; those encountered in teaching situations; those encountered in tutorial and counselling situations; those arising during day-to-day interactions with students; and those caused by students' expectations.

Any analysis of training needs uncovers a host of operational problems. The next step is to identify those problems to which training can provide a direct solution, those for which training could act as some temporary palliative while the basic causes are being remedied, and those which will not respond to training at all at this stage, since they are organizational problems, perhaps caused by unclear objectives, inappropriate systems of work, conflicting standards, or inadequate lines of communication. Being organizational problems they require organizational solutions. Only later may training be relevant, to enable staff to implement the new systems, procedures and practices created by organizational change.

Before we proceed to examine the operational difficulties identified during the research project and separate out those which are likely to respond satisfactorily to some form of training, we need to step back for a time in the analytical process. Essentially there are three main areas of investigation which combine to form an analysis of training needs and which proceed logically, one to the next, like the links in a chain: the environment in which the organization exists, its overall objectives and the plans by which it proposes to achieve those objectives, and the operational problems which it encounters in pursuit of them. We have briefly considered the latter area and will return to it. We need, however, to spend a little time considering the first two and what the implications are for the institutions concerned.

Every organization operates within a political, social and economic environment. It is affected, short or long term, by the interaction between the elements of this environment and by the interactions between the environment and itself. These interactions tend to cause change. The organization has a number of options. It can refuse to acknowledge the environment within which it is operating and remain the same as before, perhaps in the hope that the change, if ignored, will go away, perhaps from the belief that the changes are only temporary and that it is big enough and important enough in itself to ride them out. A highly likely consequence is that sooner or later the organization will cease to exist, and there are many examples within British industry over the last quarter of a century to prove the point. It can have change forced upon it, for example by government action or through market forces which compel it to react by modifying its objectives, products, services, or methods of operation in the desperate search for a strategy for survival. Or it can choose to be pro-active, looking to anticipate movements in its environment and their potential effects and to modify its own position in good time to absorb the impact of change smoothly, thereby not merely surviving but actually consolidating its position or even moving a step ahead in whatever race it is in.

The implications for universities, which arise from an examination of the environment in which they are now operating, are profound, and many of them were considered in Chapter 1. With a market-driven approach, the concept of the world as a 'customer' arises for the first time and along with it the need to convince or 'sell' as an essential strategy: from being a theoretical possibility, competition becomes a reality. The balance of power between the universities and the world shifts substantially in favour of the latter.

Secondly, if the world is a 'customer', so must the individual student be. The overseas student has considerable purchasing power; £7000 for a one-year, taught masters' degree course is no small sum and its loss to an institution is immediately noticeable. As it happens, purchasing power will no longer be restricted to overseas students. The Department of Education and Science consultation paper of April 1989, which outlines proposals to shift the balance of public funding of higher education from the block grant to fees, points out: 'by making institutions' income dependent in larger measure on their ability to attract and satisfy student demand, this funding approach will both promote effectiveness in marketing and teaching, and enhance the scope of institutional independence'.[3]

Thirdly, and inevitably, in the wake of the previous two considerations, arises the matter of competition. As has already been discussed in depth in Chapter 1, there is now considerable competition to recruit overseas students, not only between British institutions but between institutions world-wide, and it is growing. It was also pointed out in that chapter that, while competition, at least between British institutions, is at present largely subject-based, this is likely to change as universities become increasingly autonomous in their fee-charging policies, and increasingly dependent for their survival on those fees. Human nature being what it is, there will be those institutions which cut corners in order to cut costs, reduce fees and boost numbers in a bid to secure a larger share of the market. Specifically, they may reduce entry requirements to courses, reduce the level of English language competence required and deliberately tolerate a high failure rate in order to boost income. To reduce costs they may turn to the use of less skilled and experienced, and therefore cheaper, teaching and tutoring staff and omit to provide the enhanced support services which both increased numbers and the nature of overseas students' needs demand. In the short term they may well be financially successful at the expense of those institutions which maintain their academic standards.

What emerges from even a brief consideration of the increasingly commercial environment in which the universities have to operate is their urgent need for an overall strategy and sense of corporate identity, within which should be contained their decisions on a number of critical issues, among them market stance and the recruitment of overseas students. At the time of writing there is evidence that at least one university is about to attempt this.[4] The need for training may spring directly from some of these decisions. For example we found that certain staff at the two universities, who had become involved in the unfamiliar area of overseas student recruitment, were unhappy with their role. Their concern about their 'amateurishness' has already been discussed. These staff might well benefit from some training in marketing, public relations, use of the media and exhibitions work – but only after their institutions have taken some fundamental decisions about their overseas student recruitment policy. How otherwise can we ensure that those who need training are given the training they need? In many cases, these strategic decisions will not have direct training consequences. It will only be later, when they are turned into operational plans, that the training implications become more visible.

It is the operational plans, the second main area of investigation in the process of training-needs analysis, that we should now move on to consider briefly. Having decided upon its overall strategy and the objectives it wants to achieve, an organization must plan how it is going to pursue the strategy and achieve the objectives. Otherwise, it has little real control over where it is heading and merely trims its sails to take temporary advantage of whatever wind is passing. Eventually it may find itself far off-course. The operational plans will look at every aspect of the organization, covering, for example, the division of work and internal structures, allocation of resources, financial controls, systems, procedures, communication flows, and staffing and personnel policies, and should seek to provide a balance appropriate to its overall strategy between the efficiency provided by standardization and the flexibility afforded by the freedom to act autonomously.

With this as background and looking at the universities in the restricted context of their dealings with overseas students, the evidence we obtained seemed to indicate a lack of coherent yet flexible, university-wide planning. This has been discussed in depth in previous chapters. Staff experienced operational problems, arising from: the universities' practice of recruiting more overseas students while at the same time cutting back on staffing levels, financial resources and support systems; the perceived lack of university-wide policies and practices with regard to the recruitment, education and care of overseas students, resulting in a patchwork of uneven, piecemeal, departmental responses; the unsolved lack of fit between a centrally controlled, 'systems' approach and departmental autonomy; and poor horizontal communication. Now these are not problems which training can solve. Nevertheless, they must be tackled. In the light of their overall strategies and objectives, if overseas students then have a place in their plans, the institutions must review and upgrade their systems and procedures in such areas, for example, as admissions, communications, accommodation and support facilities, in order to provide a quality service. Training in the new or improved systems may then be needed.

Before leaving the investigation of the institutions' operational plans, two critical and linked issues need to be raised. The new concept of the student, not just the overseas student, as, at least in part, a 'customer' has already been discussed above. The implications are clear. 'Customers' in the last decade have come to expect good 'service'. They will have the opportunity to go elsewhere if they are not satisfied. A reputation for good quality takes a long time to gain: it can be lost overnight and then takes even longer to regain. There are sufficient examples in the automobile manufacturing industry alone to prove the point. There are many reasons for institutions to rate this issue of the utmost importance. As Juran and Gryner point out:

> A good quality reputation is a treasure. It is a matchless tool for competition by helping to obtain a better price as well as a greater volume of sales. The quality reputation also has high advertising value. Finally, the quality reputation is a morale builder because people derive much satisfaction from being on a winning industrial team.[5]

The importance of providing quality and satisfaction is not confined to manufacturing industry alone: it is of the greatest concern to all who provide a service. 'Striving for quality in all relationships and activities offers the only way an organization can prosper. Its benefits are that it:

- cuts costs and increases effectiveness by getting things right first time
- reduces waste, not just of materials but of time and all other resources
- offers the consumer what he or she needs
- results in a better service.'[6]

There was evidence also from the research project that some students and staff were also aware of the critical nature of this issue. A number of overseas students commented strongly upon the apparent lack of realization within the universities that they were in fact 'customers' and that they were entitled to 'service'. For their part, a number of staff expressed their strong concern that many overseas students did not get a fair deal and that there was an urgent need within the universities to move from negative attitudes towards the presence of overseas students to positive ones. This attitude, concerning quality of service, must permeate the whole institution. It must become the way of life, the 'mission statement'. It is not in itself a subject for training courses in the first instance. It starts from the top, from the overall strategy and the operational plans which follow. It is seen to be a reality in the way in which the institution interacts with its environment; through the quality of its strategy and planning, through the quality of its leadership and its services and ultimately through the day-to-day attitudes and behaviour of its staff. Its initial acceptance is achieved by example from the top. The first step towards total implementation is the publication of an institution's Quality Enhancement policy, in which it defines what it means by 'quality' and declares how it is going to achieve it. That done, the training needed to implement the policy can be readily identified. It might well be to the benefit of universities to contemplate such a policy.

The second, and related issue, which is critical to the planning process, concerns the expectations of overseas students, as revealed by the research project. Many of them believe that the primary function of a university is to teach and consequently arrive with the expectation that they will receive a very substantial amount of teaching, and tutorial guidance of a high quality. The evidence suggests that their expectations are not always met. The evidence also suggests that the perception among academic staff is that teaching and tutoring are not highly regarded activities within universities and do not count as criteria for promotion. The consequences of this are discussed in Chapter 2. Briefly, many staff are naturally reluctant to spend the additional time and attention, which overseas students need, on these activities, when it could be devoted to the promotion-relevant practices of research and publication. Those staff who have a commitment to teaching and tutorial work find themselves increasingly overloaded because of growing demands from students and the additional pressures caused by the reduction in staff numbers and in the support services. There is clear evidence that these staff feel that the institutions are content to take their commitment and motivation for granted while providing no recognition in return. In itself this is an unhappy state of affairs. If it is compounded with the students' desire as the 'customers' to receive high quality teaching and tutoring and on the other hand the institutions' desire to recruit more students, then the institutions have a serious problem. The solution is simple – and at this stage it is not a training one. Those who are highly skilled in teaching and tutorial work should be seen to be regarded as highly valuable assets to the institution: the proof of this will be their promotion on account of their excellence in teaching and tutoring. There will then be the motivation for other staff to acquire and demonstrate these skills and a clearly perceived need for training.

These two issues should be of the utmost concern to universities as they formulate their plans, for if students do not receive from an institution the high quality service they have a right to expect, their friends or compatriots next year will go to one that does provide it.

Having at some length set the list of operational problems with which we started into their context, it is now the appropriate point in the training-needs analysis to return to them and consider what can be done about them through the medium of staff training and development. Viewed now in the light of what has been said about the need for universities to begin to develop an overall strategy relevant to their environment and from it their operational plans, both of which processes will encompass the issues concerned with overseas students, a number of the operational problems must be removed from the list, since they are in fact organizational problems whose solution initially depends on decisions to be taken at the strategic or planning levels. They will not respond to training as a solution at this stage. When the decisions have been taken, the implications for training, at present unspecifiable, will begin to be clearer. The problems to be set aside are those which have their origins in university or departmental policies, systems or practices, as, for example, those concerned with accommodation, communication flows, and perceived institutional values. In addition the problems associated with the lack of social interaction and with cultural and dietary changes are not matters to be dealt with via a programme of staff training and development. The question of negative attitudes on the part of staff belongs partly to the whole issue of the student as the customer and the institution's policy regarding quality of service, which has been discussed above. However, aspects of it also belong to the category of day-to-day interactions and as such remain to be tackled.

From the students' viewpoint, therefore, the operational problems which staff training could immediately help to solve are: those encountered in the process of learning; those encountered in the process of interacting with staff; feelings of uncertainty and confusion; and feelings of insecurity and inferiority. The problems encountered by staff, on which training could immediately be brought to bear, comprise: those encountered in teaching situations; those encountered in tutorial and counselling situations; those arising during day-to-day interactions with students; those resulting from negative attitudes; and those caused by uncertainty about roles.

Looking again at these categories, there is a good deal of commonality between the problems encountered by students and those encountered by staff. Both parties expressed difficulties in teaching or learning situations: both parties expressed difficulties in day-to-day interactions, where attitudes and feelings are usually contributary factors. Neither party, for different reasons, was particularly happy about the way in which guidance and advice were handled. There remain the problems caused by uncertainty about roles. These were expressed by library, computer and technical staff, and centred around the issue of whether they should be simply providers of information and advice, suppliers of an end-product or trainer-facilitators. Their actual role is, of course, clearly a matter for their respective heads of department to decide. However, as there is inevitably an instructional element within the service they provide, their training needs might legitimately be considered within the area of teaching or learning situations, with additional comments in the section on guidance and advice.

At this point, before we go on to specify the actual problems encountered and use the data to examine training needs with specific reference to the two universities studied, it is essential to put that data into perspective and indicate what is meant by training needs. Of the total number of overseas students at the two universities, less than one-third contributed to our research. The proportion of staff interviewed was very much less. Moreover, it is quite possible that the minority of staff who agreed to be interviewed contained a higher proportion of those who were both concerned about the welfare of overseas students and committed to developing the relevant skills than did the rest. In other words, while we may be able with some confidence to point to certain areas of knowledge and skills as needing further development within the two institutions if they are to provide a service of quality, the actual extent of the training needs is as yet undiscovered.

Teaching and tutoring

The data provided by the research project in this category were a mixture of operational problems and perceived training needs. From the students' point of view the problems were clearly defined, and have been analysed to a greater depth in Chapter 3. There was a lack of awareness on the part of staff that many overseas students had previously only experienced formal teaching methods whereby they were expected to absorb information passively and were not expected to interact with one another or to exercise any powers of analysis on the material. To be thrust suddenly into situations where they were expected to interact, debate, find out information for themselves, and critically assesss it was bewildering. They felt that it was the responsibility of teaching staff to ease them gradually into this way of learning. Lack of constructive feedback on performance left students uncertain how to improve, particularly in the analysis of material and in written presentation. They felt that they did not receive enough advice on study skills to help them make the transition to self-responsibility and self-directed learning. They considered too that teaching staff did not really understand the difficulties of listening and writing in a foreign language.

Many of the staff interviewed were equally clear about their own training needs. They felt that they needed to improve their existing classroom teaching skills and to acquire a wider range of teaching techniques. They needed to become more skilful in conducting tutorials. They needed a greater understanding of students' learning difficulties and of the study skills required to overcome them. They thought it important to develop analytical skills to help them assess language and learning difficulties and competencies and research capabilities. Some staff, notably from the library and computer services, considered that they needed to know how to give instruction: as one member of the library staff said, 'with other overseas students I might have to take them to the index. Even then I might have to show them how the index works.' This type of observation was heard many times. The role difficulty identified by library, computer and technical staff, as to whether they should simply provide information and advice or train the students in how to use the relevant systems or actually perform the task themselves is echoed by academic staff and workshop instructors. They found that many overseas students expected solutions to be provided for them in a wide variety of situations and had difficulty at times in achieving a balance between sensitivity and firmness, between giving guidance and doing the work themselves.

From these data it is possible to draw a number of conclusions about priority areas for staff training and development within the category of teaching and tutoring. Staff would appear to need:

- To have knowledge of a wide variety of teaching techniques and skills in their use so that they are able to select and apply the one which is most appropriate to the experience of their students and the material being taught.
- An understanding of how people learn, of the different preferred styles of learning and of study skills so that they are able to identify individual learning difficulties and give advice on how to overcome them.
- To develop further their classroom lecturing skills, with particular emphasis on structuring of the material, clarity of delivery, and the use of visual aids.
- To develop the skills of giving task instruction.
- An understanding of why, how and when to give constructive feedback and practice in doing so.
- An understanding of the steps involved in a systematic approach to problem specification and analysis.

Staff have a difficult balance to maintain. On the one hand they have to instruct, teach, correct, and give advice and direction: on the other hand they need to set boundaries, avoid student dependency, encourage self-responsibility and promote critical thinking. One tutor summed this up very clearly:

> Teaching staff need training in how to move students from a state of dependency, how to get students talking and discussing, how to encourage Muslim women students to participate in male-dominated groups, how to get students to exercise self-responsibility. These things should not be left to chance.

What we are talking about, in fact, are the skills of facilitating learning in just about every context apart from the formal lecture, and they are as relevant to those librarians, computer staff and technicians with uncertainties over what role they should play as they are to the academic staff and workshop instructors. We should therefore add to the list of priority areas one more, with the highest priority of all:

- Facilitator skills, with particular reference to why, when, when not to, and how to make training interventions.

Because of the particular importance of this aspect of staff training within this category, the programme for a training course in Facilitator Skills, which the author has developed and used, is given below, in the hope that it may provide some ideas for others to take further.

FACILITATOR SKILLS PROGRAMME

Day 1

AFTERNOON

Introduction and delegates' objectives:

Who; Where from; Other training done;
Types of facilitation undertaken.
The role of the Facilitator:

What is facilitating)	Group discussion
)	facilitated by tutors.
Why do it)	(Videotaped).
)	
When not to do it)	Material to be
)	collated into a
How to do it)	handout.

What skills do you need to facilitate?
(Videotaped).
Skills Input:
   Listening Skills
   The use of Body Language
   Questioning Skills

FACILITATING RETROSPECTIVE EXAMINATION

EVENING

Examination of tutors' facilitation on videotape. (Tutors to collect items of good and bad practice to generate into a handout.) Tutors to lead off and then two delegates to facilitate group in turn. (Delegates are videotaped).

Day 2

MORNING

Skills Input:

Making Interventions:
   Why; When; When Not To:
   Styles of Intervention and Criteria for Selection
   Giving feedback →

MORNING
&
AFTERNOON

Examination of delegates' facilitation of previous evening's videotape. Two delegates to facilitate group in turn. (Tutors continue collating data for compilation into a handout. Delegates are videotaped.)
The process of facilitation/videotaping/facilitated examination of videotape continues until all delegates have facilitated and received feedback.

EVENING   Input on Group Dynamics
                   Briefing on overnight work – each delegate to facilitate a
                   session on e.g.:
                        'Responsibility for learning'
                        'Expectations from learners of their facilitators'
                        'Uses of various types of interventions'
                        'Confrontation'
                        'How does a facilitator add value?'
                        'Limitations of structure'
                   or other issues as appropriate to the group's learning.

                   FACILITATING THE 'HERE AND NOW'
Day 3   Group Dynamics examination group (videotaped and
MORNING   facilitated by two delegates in turn)
   &   Examination of delegates' facilitation using videotape
AFTERNOON   (facilitated by delegates individually)
                   Review/feedback on facilitations
                   20-minute facilitations by delegates on topics prepared from
                   previous evening.
AFTERNOON   Review/feedback on facilitations.
                   Unfinished business – review programme against delegates'
                   objectives for the course.
                   Questionnaires and Action plan.

Day-to-day interactions

The incidence of problems, difficulties and training needs, expressed both by
students and staff, which fall within this category, far exceeds all others
combined. This in itself would indicate that the highest priority be given to the
training needs which emerge from this section. It should not, however, be taken to
suggest that relationships between staff and students are disastrously bad.
True, the cultural differences and perceptions between people of different
nations can turn an unsatisfactory communication into a total misunderstand-
ing. Nevertheless, in order to keep the situation in perspective, it should be
realized that the nature and extent of the interpersonal problems we unearthed
were not greatly different from those one might find in any place in the United
Kingdom where people have to work together.

   Students attributed the difficulties they encountered primarily to the following factors: the reactive, rather than pro-active, behaviour of staff (in other
words, many staff did not make the first move towards establishing a relationship with students but waited for the students to come to them); a lack of
background knowledge of the countries from which the students came; a lack of
understanding of what it is like to be on one's own, studying in a foreign country
(to put it another way, a lack of empathy, an inability or unwillingness to see a
situation from the other person's point of view); not seeming to be listened to;

arrogance and prejudice on the part of staff; stereotyping; the treatment of mature students as juveniles; and a wide variety of personal feelings, which staff did not appear to pick up, such as inadequacy, loss of status, confusion, insecurity, embarrassment and the fear of losing face.

For their part, staff expressed a mixture of interactive difficulties and perceived training needs. In all categories of staff, other than academic, some of those interviewed spoke of the lower status accorded them by some students and of arrogant attitudes encountered. Many female staff, particularly secretarial, library and computing, spoke of aggressive and imperious behaviour on the part of, mostly male, students; 'male chauvinism' was a term frequently used. Many staff, particularly administrative and secretarial, told of having to deal with frustration and aggression when students either did not understand what was explained to them or found that there were systems and procedures to be followed. Dealing with attempts to bribe, barter and exploit was another difficult situation to handle. On the more positive side, staff spoke of other difficulties, of dealing with students' feelings of insecurity and fear of loss of face, in particular the face-saving 'yes' when the student did not in fact understand. Many were well aware that students encountered arrogance, stereotyping and patronizing behaviour from staff. The observations of a library assistant summarize well much of what was heard:

> We do seem to be exposed in the library to the effects of cultural differences. Some overseas students seem to approach us expecting to be disadvantaged. Their insecurities can produce aggression. Also, all the counter staff are women. They are often treated imperiously by male overseas students. 'Please' is a word absent from their vocabulary. The face-saving 'yes' is also hard to cope with when accompanied by a non-comprehending expression.

Difficult situations arising from living arrangements were encountered in addition to those arising from work, situations which are explored in Chapter 4. As well as being on the receiving end of often imperious complaints about facilities, staff found themselves having to ensure fair play, defuse cultural and racial tensions between students, and be a source of advice or comfort to individuals. Here, residential and domestic staff were in the front line, yet had received no training in how to handle such potentially difficult interactions.

Not surprisingly, staff had a clear perception of their overall training needs, though they were often uncertain as to how the needs might be met. The most commonly expressed desire was for training in interpersonal, or communications, skills. The usefulness of knowing about the different backgrounds and experiences of students was stressed, as was the importance of becoming more aware of and sensitive to their needs and of showing that awareness. Giving support, respect and praise were considered essential, showing concern for them as people. The comments of a laboratory technician, with many years of experience, summarize the approach which many staff were seeking.

> It's a matter of respect for others. I have learned that it is a job to make sure students understand the first time round. I have to be sensitive to their

position and their status, for they may be of a very high status in their own
country, and feel embarrassed at finding it difficult to understand something new here. It's a matter of being courteous and showing understanding and respect for every student according to his different needs.

It is clearly not feasible to try to equip every member of staff with the
background knowledge of all the countries from which students come, all the
problems they might face, and all the needs they might have. Instead we should
concentrate on helping them to develop general knowledge and skills which they
will be able to apply widely and effectively to any particular situation; in other
words, they will have learned how to handle situations rather than all the
answers. A programme of interpersonal skills training is the recommended
solution. Such a programme should contain the following elements:

The 'philosophy' behind the programme:

- That participants already possess most of the knowledge and skills they need
  by virtue of the fact that they have been operating in society effectively for
  many years. This helps to put the training in perspective and reduce the
  feelings of insecurity or hostility which are sometimes present at the start of
  such programmes.
- That the programme is therefore very much concerned with pulling together
  and formalizing existing knowledge and skills as well as offering some
  possibly new ideas.
- That the overall purpose is to increase awareness of our own behaviour, the
  reasons for that behaviour, and the effect it has upon others. That behaviour
  breeds behaviour.
- That when we are aware of our behaviour and its effects upon others, we can
  control it and eventually, if we wish, choose to behave differently.

Fundamental communications skills:

- Listening
- Observation and use of body language
- Questioning
- Practical exercises in each of the above

An understanding of the communication process:

- In particular, the parts which feelings, motives, attitudes including stereotyping, and interpretation can play in distorting the process.

Frameworks to help in the application of the knowledge and skills:

- The knowledge of and skill in using one or more theoretical frameworks can
  be particularly helpful in the heat of a stressful interaction such as dealing
  with male chauvinism, aggression, arrogance, exploitation, or indeed insecurity and confusion, whether it is the student's or one's own. A framework
  offers a way of taking the individual, seemingly unrelated, elements of a
  communication and fitting them together into a pattern of action and
  reaction that makes sense. We are then in a better position to control at least

our part in that interaction and direct it into more positive and productive ways.

- One such framework is Assertiveness Training, well described, albeit unknowingly, by a departmental secretary: 'I try to maintain a steady insistence on ways of proceeding here whilst recognizing the early difficulties experienced by some cultures in accepting these.'
- Another model, often taught in conjunction with Assertiveness, is Trans-actional Analysis, to the depth of second-level structural analysis.
- Practical exercises in the application of the frameworks, based on partici-pants' own experiences.

The development by each participant by the end of the programme of a personal action plan for increasing their interpersonal skills, in order to help achieve a transfer of the learning from the classroom to the work situation.

Such a programme must be available to all staff in the institution who need it. Rather than restrict a particular programme to a particular category of staff, it is strongly recommended that it contains a mix of participants from different functions, since this affords an almost unique opportunity for additional learning of, and from, the difficulties encountered by colleagues in other areas of work.

One of the numerous interpersonal skills programmes which the author has developed and run is outlined below to illustrate one way of fitting together the elements which have been described. The programme ran on one evening per week for five weeks, each session lasting three hours, with twelve participants as the ideal number.

SESSION 1
- Introduction, Objectives and Outline of Programme and 'Philosophy'
- 'Ice-breaker' exercise to effect personal introductions
- Handout of 'Personal Development Inventory', to be filled in by participants as the programme progresses
- Listening Skills:
    Discussion, Exercises in Pairs and Fours and Review
- The Observation and Use of Body Language:
    Discussion, Exercises in Pairs and Fours and Review
- Questioning Skills:
    Discussion, Exercises in Threes and Review
- Review of the session, completion of individual 'Skills Sheet' and issue of 'homework' on 'Individual Action Plans'.

SESSION 2
- Review and discussion of 'homework', in Fours
- 'Putting the Skills Together':
    Role-Plays, Feedback and Discussion, in Fours, to practise and consolidate the skills
- Barriers to Communication:

Discussion of the ways in which Feelings, Motives, Attitudes and Perceptions can distort Communications
A model to illustrate the process and Worked Examples
- The 'Philosophy' expanded:
  Where we're starting from
  Where we're going to
  How we might get there
  Awareness to Control to Choice
  The usefulness of Frameworks
- Review of the session and issue of 'homework' sheets to identify 'Situations I'd Like to Be Able to Change'.

SESSION 3
- Framework 1 – Assertiveness:
  Classification of Behaviours and associated Body Language
  Saying 'No' without Apologizing: Exercises in Threes and Review
  Plenary group review of pressures and difficulties experienced
  'Declaration of Rights' and discussion
- Techniques for Assertiveness:
  Being Persistent:
    - Setting Objectives and Fall-Back Positions
    - 'Broken Record': description then practice in Threes and Review
  Coping with Criticism:
    - 'Fogging': description then practice in Threes and Review
    - 'Negative Enquiry': description then practice in Threes and Review
- Review of the session and issue of 'homework' sheets 'Steps Towards Assertiveness', building on the previous session's 'homework'.

SESSION 4
- Assertiveness (continued):
  Major exercises in Fours, using the personal situations generated and developed in the two previous sets of 'homework', to practise collectively and consolidate Assertiveness techniques: group reviews
  Plenary group review of Assertiveness and resolution of difficulties
- Framework 2 – Transactional Analysis:
  Background, Purpose and Applications
  First-Level Structural Analysis: Description and Worked Examples
  Second-Level Structural Analysis: Description and Worked Examples
  Tie-in with Assertiveness
- Review of second part of session and issue of 'homework' sheets for the application of Structural Analysis to the personal situations previously identified.

SESSION 5
- Transactional Analysis (continued):
  Plenary group review of any issues or difficulties arising from the 'homework'

Major exercises, in new groups of Four, using the personal situations to practise and consolidate the use of Structural Analysis, together with Assertiveness Techniques: group reviews
Plenary group review of Transactional Analysis and resolution of difficulties
- Review of whole programme and completion of individual 'Personal Development Inventory' sheets
- Issue and individual completion of 'Personal Action Plan' sheet. Plans shared and discussed in Pairs or Threes.

Guidance and advice

Within this category also the research project revealed a mixture of operational problems and perceived solutions. Students commented particularly on the reluctance of many academic staff to assume the responsibility for making the initial approach to the relationship, on the lack of personal time and attention given by academic staff, on their lack of knowledge of the students' home background and on their inability or unwillingness to see through the eyes of a stranger the systems and practices so familiar to themselves. The last criticism was also directed at library, computing and technical staff when help with specialist services was required. Students were equally forthright concerning solutions. They felt that it was up to staff to take the initiative, since staff were the people with both the knowledge and the authority. They considered that the most important factor was the early establishment of personal rapport, leading to an interactive relationship and a supportive attitude which would give them the confidence to proceed. In the early stages of the relationship there should be a clear structure with directive guidance and comprehensive feedback; over a period of time appropriate to the student's development, the relationship would gradually move from dependence and supervision to selfresponsibility and self-assessment. Guidance and advice should be practical and specific, not vague and general, because uncertainty in the early stages tended to produce depression or even alienation.

In many respects, the dilemma of the staff position was encapsulated in the comments of one tutor:

> It is vital to go to the student to offer practical help and pre-empt the formation of problems. Once they realize that I am available many come, really seeking reassurance. A strange environment, culture shock and the extra pressures to succeed which go with paying huge fees all cause loss of confidence. Tutors must 'read between the lines' but this all takes a lot of time.

Apart from the heavy demands made on already inadequate time, staff identified a number of other difficulties. Overseas students tended to want to relate to one person only in a particular environment and could become upset or withdrawn if that person were not available, even when support was offered. Helping students to cope with family problems or tragedies was a particularly stressful matter for staff involved, the majority of whom might well have received no training at all in such work. As one chaplain said: 'We cannot just ignore this involvement. When a relative dies, for example, their reaction may be stronger than we might anticipate and they need tremendous support.'

Picking up the theme of training for a moment, we have already noted the front-line role of residential and domestic staff in providing advice and comfort to individual students: we could add secretarial and other staff to the list of informal helpers, none of whom had received any relevant training to enable them to handle delicate situations. A number of staff, particularly in the counselling and health-care services, raised the problem of the 'wrapped-up' request for help. As one doctor commented: 'Overseas students do take much more of our time, not so much because of language difficulties but because of anxiety and inhibitions. They hesitate to come to the point or they assign physical symptoms to stress-related problems.' There then follows the very complex and time-consuming task of unearthing the real problem. The situation was echoed by a personal tutor who said, 'More and more [students] fall into the mature category. They find asking for help particularly difficult because of their upbringing.'

Nor is there necessarily any clear resolution. We have already noted the tendency of some overseas students to expect solutions to be provided for them: counsellors also reported that students could become disillusioned if immediate solutions to complex problems were not forthcoming. At the same time, the solution had to be culturally acceptable to the student: the comment of the doctor quoted above, concerning stress-related problems, continued: 'Because many overseas students have different methods of disease analysis, it is difficult to make recommendations. Any suggestion that a student is "not coping" carries a stigma.' The final difficulty is one we have met before in another category concerning the uncertainty on the part of support staff as to when to take charge of a student's learning and when to be simply supportive. Nevertheless, throughout all these difficulties, many of the staff interviewed remained aware of their own needs for development: for greater understanding of and sensitivity towards signs of problems and stress among their students, for a wider knowledge of sources and help both inside and outside the universities, and for the constant need to be non-judgemental.

Although the list of operational difficulties is lengthy and the nature of many of them complex, the part which training can play in resolving them is relatively simple to describe. The main prerequisite is that the motivation should be there. The basic conditions for this, namely the concept of the student as a 'customer', the total commitment of the institution to quality of service and, as a consequence, its high regard for tutoring and counselling skills, have been discussed previously and will be assumed. There is, in fact, a considerable overlap between this and the other categories of training need already dealt with. The basic skills essential for handling satisfactorily the majority of situations described in this section are the same as those considered essential for successful day-to-day interaction: the ability to listen, the ability to observe and use body language, and the ability to ask effective questions. These are in fact the basic skills of counselling. For those staff whose work may also involve them in the initial handling of particularly complex or stressful situations, such as personal tutors, hall wardens and domestic staff, additional training in counselling skills is important. Essentially this is counselling with a small 'c', the type of training which managers and supervisors in industrial and other organizations have received for some time, and is not intended to supplant the professional counsellor. The basic premise is that the manager or supervisor has an initial responsibility for the care of their staff: the parallel with the university situation is clear. The objectives of such training should be to:

- enable staff to give initial and immediate help
- ensure that staff are fully aware of sources of professional help inside and outside the institution
- enable staff to know when they should refer the student to professional sources of help and what source to contact
- enable staff to know how to keep post-counselling contact with the student

Such courses should be organized and run by the institution's own professional counselling staff and should clearly contain a large element of practical exercises and role-plays using real-life material suitably disguised. A further overlap with other categories of training occurs in the case of the face-saving 'yes'. The comments of the students who used this technique throw a revealing light on the situation. Those for whom a situation was wholly new said that they could only ask so many questions before they began to feel demoralized and stupid. They had therefore said 'yes' even though they had not in fact understood. This situation could be remedied by the use of some form of exercise to test understanding and pick up any deficiencies. It might also be identified by the practised application of the basic skills of questioning, listening and observing. It could be avoided in the first place through familiarity on the part of the staff concerned with the basic principles of task instruction, the first one of which is to break the task down to start with into component parts which can be assimilated readily in one piece of instruction, thereby avoiding overloading the learner.

One final suggestion for staff development within this category remains to be mentioned. A composite picture of the ideal supervisor or personal tutor was built up from students' proposed solutions to the problems they faced and was described at length in Chapter 3 and outlined in the first part of this section. It is essentially concerned with the stages in the development of the supervisor–student relationship and as such bears a remarkable resemblance to the theory of Situational Leadership which has found considerable application in the training of industrial managers and supervisors. There is no need to go to the length of providing a special training course in the theory but supervisors and tutors might find it interesting and useful reading.[7]

During the course of this chapter a lot of ground has been covered and many suggestions for training and development have been made. It might be useful,

Categories of staff	Knowledge needed	Skills needed
Academic	Teaching techniques	Use of appropriate techniques
	Methods and styles of learning	
	Study skills	
	Principles of effective presentation	Lecturing and presentation
	Principles of effective feedback	Giving appropriate feedback
	Systematic approach to problem specification	Problem specification and analysis
	Facilitator skills	Use of appropriate facilitator skills
	Interpersonal skills	Use of appropriate IP skills
(tutors, wardens)	Counselling skills	Use of appropriate counselling skills
(tutors, supervisors)	Situational leadership	
Administrative	Interpersonal skills	Use of appropriate IP skills
Clerical and secretarial	Interpersonal skills	Use of appropriate IP skills
Computer	Principles of task instruction	Giving effective task instruction
	Principles of effective feedback	Giving appropriate feedback
	Systematic approach to problem specification	Problem specification and analysis
	Facilitator skills	Use of appropriate facilitator skills
	Interpersonal skills	Use of appropriate IP skills
Domestic and residential	Interpersonal skills	Use of appropriate IP skills
	Counselling skills	Use of appropriate counselling skills
Health care	Interpersonal skills	Use of appropriate IP skills
	Counselling skills	Use of appropriate counselling skills
Instructor	Principles of task instruction	Giving effective task instruction
	Principles of effective feedback	Giving appropriate feedback
	Facilitator skills	Use of appropriate facilitator skills
	Interpersonal skills	Use of appropriate IP skills
Library	Principles of task instruction	Giving effective task instruction

therefore, to summarize these suggestions by category of staff in alphabetical order, before closing.

Categories of staff	Knowledge needed	Skills needed
	Principles of effective feedback	Giving appropriate feedback
	Systematic approach to problem specification	Problem specification and analysis
	Facilitator skills	Use of appropriate facilitator skills
	Interpersonal skills	Use of appropriate IP skills
Technical	Principles of task instruction	Giving effective task instruction
	Principles of effective feedback	Giving appropriate feedback
	Facilitator skills	Use of appropriate facilitator skills
	Interpersonal skills	Use of appropriate IP skills

Earlier in this chapter mention was made that the research project did not set out to be an analysis of staff training needs in itself but an investigation into the experiences of overseas students at two universities. It did reveal operational problems and through these gave an insight into the further knowledge and skills which staff who are dealing with overseas students need. As an analysis of training needs, however, it is incomplete and the investigation would need to be taken further. We have a composite picture of what staff need to know and be able to do. What we do not know is how precisely existing staff compare with that picture. In other words, as has been indicated earlier, we know the areas in which training is needed but we do not know the extent of it. We would need to assess the existing stock of knowledge and skills which staff involved possess, taking into account their previous training and experience, and compare that stock against what we have identified as necessary for them to have. The difference between the two represents the extent of the training need. There is, after all, no point in training staff in knowledge and skills they already adequately possess. The next step would be to prepare a plan to meet those training needs, identifying specific priority areas for training, both in terms of competencies and staff groups, together with the costs involved and the resources needed. The plan should be the blueprint from which programmes of training and development are prepared to meet participants' needs. At this stage we should need to decide on content, duration and training methods appropriate to the competencies required, the participants and the time available, select and, if necessary, train the trainers and identify, wherever possible, the desired standards of performance by which we would subsequently evaluate the training.

As can be appreciated, therefore, a considerable amount of work still remains to be done before we can actually say that we have a precise knowledge of the training needs of staff at the two universities concerned whose work involves them with overseas students and state how precisely we should plan to meet those needs. What we do have is a fairly clear idea of where the priority training needs lie. The work we have done may serve as a convenient starting point for those in other institutions who wish to investigate their own situation in order ultimately to improve the quality of the service provided for the overseas student.

References

1. J. R. Talbot and C. D. Ellis *Analysis and Costing of Company Training*, London, Gower Press, 1969. p. 17.
2. B. M. Bass and J. A. Vaughan *Training in Industry*, Belmont, Calif., Wadsworth, 1969. p. 73.
3. Department of Education and Science, 'Shifting the balance of public funding of higher education to fees'. *Department of Education and Science Consultation Paper*, April 1989, p. 2, section 4a.
4. 'Surrey sees market vision': *The Times Higher Educational Supplement*, 863, 19 May 1989, p. 3.
5. J. M. Juran and F. M. Gryna Jr. *Quality Planning and Analysis*, New York, McGraw-Hill, 1970, pp. 534–5.
6. Shropshire Health Authority. *Draft Quality Enhancement Policy*: Shrewsbury, Shropshire Health Authority, March 1989, section 1.6.
7. P. Hersey and K. H. Blanchard *Management of Organizational Behaviour: Utilizing Human Resources*, 3rd edn, Englewood Cliffs, NJ, Prentice-Hall, 1977.

Bibliography

Animashawun, G. (1963). 'African students in Britain', *Race*, 5, 38–47.

Armenio, J. (1978). 'Back to the Agora: marketing foreign admissions', *Journal of the National Association of College Admissions Counsellors*, 22, 30–4.

Association of University Teachers/United Kingdom Council for Overseas Student Affairs (1986). *Responsible Recruitment: Report of a Conference. Feb. 20 1986*, London.

Banjo, G. (1975). 'Cultural castration', *UKCOSA News* 7, 14–18.

Barty, A. (1985). 'Meeting the needs of overseas students', *AUT Bulletin*, May, 18.

Bass, B. M. and Vaughan, J. A. (1969). *Training in Industry*, Belmont, Calif., Wadsworth.

Beltz, S. (1986). 'For all matters concerning overseas students', *Association of Commonwealth Universities Bulletin of Current Documentation*, 75, 16–17.

Berrill, Sir K. (1987). *The Next Steps. Report of an Advisory Committee of the Overseas Students Trust*, London, Overseas Students Trust.

British Council (1980). *Study Modes and Academic Development of Overseas Students*, London.

British Council (1985). *Higher Education Market Survey. Jordan*, London.

British Council (1985). *Higher Education Market Survey. Singapore*, London.

British Council (1986). *Higher Education Market Survey, Thailand*, London.

Brown, G. A. and Atkins, M. (1988). *Effective Teaching in Higher Education*, London, Methuen.

Burns, D. (ed.) (1965). *Travelling Scholars: an Enquiry into the Adjustment and Attitudes of Overseas Students holding Commonwealth Bursaries in England and Wales*, Slough, National Foundation for Educational Research.

Campbell, V. (1974). *Communication Problems of Overseas Students in British Technical Education*, London, N.E. London Polytechnic.

Carlas, Y. (1966). 'Some sources of reading problems in foreign language learners', in A. Smith (ed.), *Communication and Culture*, New York, Holt, Rinehart, Winston.

Carnegie Council on Policy Studies in Higher Education (1979). *Fair Practice in Higher Education*, San Francisco, Jossey-Bass.

Carswell, J. (1985). *Government and the Universities in Britain: Programme and Performance*, Cambridge, Cambridge University Press.

Committee of Vice-Chancellors and Principals (1985). *Postgraduate Training and Research*, London.

Committee of Vice-Chancellors and Principals (1985). *Report of the Steering Committee for Efficiency Studies in Universities* (The Jarratt Report), London.

Committee of Vice-Chancellors and Principals (1986). *Academic Standards in Universities*, London.

Commonwealth Standing Committee on Student Mobility (1986). *Fifth Report. Common-*

wealth Student Mobility: Commitment and Resources. London, Commonwealth Secretariat.

Cowell, R. (1982). 'Education gets the soap-powder treatment', *Times Higher Education Supplement*, 4 June, 13.

Cowie, A. P. and Heaton, J. B. (eds) (1975). *English for Academic Purposes*, Reading, BAAL/SELMOUS, University of Reading.

Cross, A. (1975). 'Russian students in eighteenth-century Oxford', *Journal of European Studies*, 5, 91–116.

Davies, S. and West, R. (1984). *The Pitman Guide to English Language Examinations*, London, Pitman Education.

Department of Education and Science (1989). Shifting the balance of public funding of higher education to fees. *Department of Education and Science Consultation Paper*, April.

Dore, R. (1976). *The Diploma Disease*, London, Unwin Education.

Dunlop, F. (1966). *Europe's Guests, Students and Trainees: a Survey on the Welfare of Foreign Students and Trainees in Europe*, Strasbourg, Council for Cultural Co-operation, Council of Europe.

Findlayson, J. (ed.) (1985). 'Developing a policy for recruiting overseas students', *Coombe Lodge Report*, 17.

Fransson, L. (1985). 'Internationalizing the universities', in *Proceedings of the 25th Anniversary AIR Forum, Promoting Excellence through Information and Technology. Portland, Oregon, April 28–May 1, 1985*. Portland, Oregon, Association for Institutional Research.

Frijhoff, W. (1976). 'Etudiants hollandais dans les collèges français aux 17 et 18 siècles, *Lias*, 3, 301–12.

Frijhoff, W. (1977). 'Etudiants étrangers à l'académie d'Angers au 17 siècle', *Lias*, 4, 13–84.

Geoghegan, G. (1983). *Non-native Speakers of English at Cambridge University*, Cambridge, Bell Education Trust.

Greenall, G. M. and Price, J. E. (eds) (1980). *Study Modes and Academic Development of Overseas Students* (ELT Documents 109), London, British Council.

Hersey, P. and Blanchard, K. H. (1977). *Management of Organizational Behavior: Utilizing Human Resources*, 3rd edn, Englewood Cliffs, NJ, Prentice-Hall.

James G. (ed.) (1984). 'The ESP classroom', *Exeter Linguistic Studies*, 17.

Jenkins, H. M. (1983). *Educating Students from Other Nations*, San Francisco, Jossey-Bass.

Juran, J. M. and Gryna, F. M. (1970). *Quality Planning and Analysis*, New York, McGraw-Hill.

Kendall, M. (1968). *Overseas Students and their Families: a Study at a London College*, London, Research Unit for Students' Problems.

Kendall, M. (1968). *Overseas Students in Britain: an Annotated Bibliography*, London, Research Unit for Students' Problems/the United Kingdom Council for Overseas Student Affairs.

Kinnell, M. (1989). 'International marketing in UK higher education: some issues in relation to marketing educational programmes to students', *European Journal of Marketing*, 23 (5), 7–21.

Kleinberg, O. and Hull, W. (1979). *At a Foreign University. An International Study of Adaptation and Coping*, New York, Praeger.

Kotler, P. (1975). *Marketing for Non-profit Organizations*, Englewood Cliffs, NJ, Prentice-Hall.

Kotler, P. (1976). 'Applying marketing theory to college admissions', in *A Role for Marketing in College Admissions. Proceedings of the Colloquium on College Admissions, Fontana, Wisconsin. May 16–18, 1976*, New York, College Entrance Examination Board.

Lee-Warner, Sir W. (1922). *Report of the Committee on Indian Students, 1907. Appendix IV of the Lytton Committee Report, Part I*, London, HMSO, for the India Office.

Lewis, I. (1984). *The Student Experience of Higher Education – University of York*, London, Croom Helm.

Litten, L. (1980). 'Marketing higher education. Benefits and risks for the American academic system', *Journal of Higher Education*, 51, 40–59.

Livingstone, A. (1960). *The Overseas Student in Britain*, Manchester, Manchester University Press.

Loughborough University of Technology (1987). *The Academic Plan to 1990: the First Phase of a Longer Term Strategy*, Loughborough.

Lovelock, C. H. (1979). 'Theoretical contributions from services and non-business marketing', in O. C. Ferrell, S. W. Brown and C. W. Lamb, *Conceptual and Theoretical Developments in Marketing*, Chicago, American Marketing Association.

Lovelock, C. H. and Rothschild, M. L. (1980). 'Uses, abuses and misuses of marketing in higher education', in *Marketing in College Admissions: a Broadening of Perspectives*, New York, College Entrance Examination Board.

McAleese, R. and Welsh, J. (1983). 'The supervision of postgraduate research students' in J. F. Eggleston and S. Delamont (eds), *The Supervision of Students for Research Degrees*, Birmingham, BERA.

McDonagh, J. and French, A. (eds) (1981). *The ESP Teacher: Role, Development and Prospects* (ELT Documents 112), London, British Council.

Mackey, M. (1980). 'The selling of the sheepskin', *Change*, 12, 28–33.

Majaro, S. (1977). *International Marketing: a Strategic Approach to World Markets*, London, Allen & Unwin.

Performance Indicator Steering Committee (1987). *University Management Information and Performance Indicator Statistics*, London, Committee of Vice-Chancellors and Principals.

Perren, G. (1963). 'The linguistic problems of overseas students', *ETIC Occasional Paper*, no. 3, London, British Council.

Political and Economic Planning (1954). 'Students from the colonies', *Planning*, 20, 374.

Political and Economic Planning (1965). *New Commonwealth Students in Britain*, London.

Price, J. (ed.) (1978). *Pre-sessional English Language Courses in Britain Today*, Newcastle on Tyne, University of Newcastle/SELMOUS/ETIC.

Reed, B., Hutton, J. and Bazalgette, J. (1978). *Freedom to Study: Requirements of Overseas Students in the UK*, London, Overseas Students Trust.

Robinson, P. (ed.) (1988). *Academic Writing: Process and Product* (ELT Documents 129), London, Macmillan.

Rogers, K. (1984). 'Foreign students: economic benefit or liability?', *College Board Review*, 133, 20–5.

Sen, A. (1970). *Problems of Overseas Students and Nurses*, Slough, National Foundation for Educational Research.

Sharp, T. E. (1982). 'Institutional administration and the foreign student program', *College and University*, 57, 323–6.

Shotnes, S. (ed.) (1985). *The Teaching and Tutoring of Overseas Students*, London, United Kingdom Council for Overseas Student Affairs.

Shotnes, S. (ed.) (1986). *International Comparisons in Overseas Student Affairs*, London, United Kingdom Council for Overseas Student Affairs.

Shropshire Health Authority (1989). *Draft Quality Enhancement Policy*, Shrewsbury, March.

Singh, A. (1963). *Indian Students in Britain*, London, Asia Publishing House.

Stewart, G. (1979). 'British students at the University of Göttingen in the eighteenth century', *German Life and Letters*, 33, 24–41.

Stone, S. (1985). 'Developing a marketing strategy', *Coombe Lodge Report*, 17, 679–84.

Talbot, J. R. and Ellis, C. D. (1969). *Analysis and Costing of Company Training*, London, Gower Press.

Times Higher Education Supplement (1989). 'Surrey sees market vision', *Times Higher Education Supplement*, 863, May 19.

Thomas, R. E. (1974). 'So you want to recruit foreign students?', *Journal of the National Association of College Admissions Counsellors*, 19, 11–12.

United Kingdom Council for Overseas Student Affairs (1989). *Language and Study Skills*, London.

Walker, D. (1985). 'Hard-sell recruiting by British universities assailed', *Chronicle of Higher Education*, 30, 39–40.

Watt, D. (1980). 'Scottish student life abroad in the fourteenth century', *Scottish Historical Review*, 59, 3–21.

Williams, G., Woodhall, M. and O'Brien, U. (1986). *Overseas Students and their Place of Study: Report of a Survey*, London, Overseas Students Trust.

Williams, P. (1982). *A Policy for Overseas Students*, London, Overseas Students Trust.

Wright, J. (1982). *Learning to Learn in Higher Education*, London, Croom Helm.

Wright, J. (1985). 'Intercultural postgraduate learning, the acquisition of study skills: an institutional response to the results of research', *International Journal for the Advancement of Counselling*, 8, 279–96.

Wright, J. (1986). 'The acquisition of research skills by postgraduates in UK universities: cognitive development in interactive settings', *Canadian Journal of Counselling*, April.

Index

The Society for Research into Higher Education

The Society exists both to encourage and co-ordinate research and development into all aspects of Higher Education, including academic, organizational and policy issues; and also to provide a forum for debate – verbal and printed.

The Society's income derives from subscriptions, book sales, conference fees and grants. It receives no subsidies and is wholly independent. Its corporate members are institutions of higher education, research institutions and professional, industrial, and governmental bodies. Its individual members include teachers and researchers, administrators and students. Members are found in all parts of the world and the Society regards its international work as amongst its most important activities.

The Society discusses and comments on policy, organizes conferences and encourages research. Under the imprint SRHE & OPEN UNIVERSITY PRESS, it is a specialist publisher, having some 40 titles in print. It also publishes *Studies in Higher Education* (three times a year) which is mainly concerned with academic issues; *Higher Education Quarterly* (formerly *Universities Quarterly*) mainly concerned with policy issues; *Abstracts* (three times a year); an *International Newsletter* (twice a year) and *SRHE News* (four times a year).

The Society's committees, study groups and branches are run by members (with help from a small secretariat at Guildford), and aim to provide a forum for discussion. The groups at present include a Teacher Education Study Group, a Staff Development Group, a Women in Higher Education Group and a Continuing Education Group each of which may have their own organization, subscriptions or publications (e.g. the *Staff Development Newsletter*). A further Questions of Quality Group has organized a series of Anglo-American seminars in the USA and the UK.

The Governing Council, elected by members, comments on current issues; and discusses policies with leading figures, notably at its evening Forums. The Society organizes seminars on current research, and is in touch with bodies in the UK such as the NAB, CVCP, UGC, CNAA and with sister-bodies overseas. It cooperates with the British Council on courses run in conjunction with its conferences.

The Society's conferences are often held jointly and have considered 'Standards and Criteria in Higher Education' (1986, with Bulmershe College); 'Restructuring' (1987, with the City of Birmingham Polytechnic); 'Academic Freedom' (1988, the University of Surrey). In 1989, 'Access and Institutional Change' (with the Polytechnic of North London). In 1990 the topic will be 'Industry and Higher Education' (with the University of Surrey). In 1991 the topic will be 'Research in Higher Education'. Other conferences have considered the DES 'Green Paper' (1985) 'HE after the Election' (1987) and 'After the Reform Act' (1988). An annual series on 'The First-Year Experience' with the University of South Carolina and Teesside Polytechnic held two meetings in 1988 in

Cambridge, and another in St Andrew's in July 1989. For some of the Society's conferences, special studies are commissioned in advance, as 'Precedings'.

Members receive free of charge the Society's *Abstracts*, annual conference Proceedings (or 'Precedings'), *SHRE News and International Newsletter* and may buy SRHE & OPEN UNIVERSITY PRESS books at discount and *Higher Education Quarterly* on special terms. Corporate members also receive the Society's journal *Studies in Higher Education* free (individuals on special terms). Members may also obtain certain other journals at a discount, including the NFER *Register of Educational Research*. There is a substantial discount to members, and to staff of corporate members, on annual and some other conference fees.

Further information from SRHE at the University, Guildford, GU2 5XH.